"Auron MacIntyre belongs to a younger set of serious, intellectually independent thinkers on the right, who are destined to have a profound impact on American political culture. It is hard to read Auron's work without noticing his obvious strengths. Unlike many others of his generation who speak for 'American conservatism,' Auron is broadly educated and strikingly literate. He is also widely read in, among other subjects, political and social theory and draws on a wide range of thinkers, starting with Plato and Aristotle, to examine what he aptly describes as the 'total state.' And to his credit, he never minces words in getting to the heart of the matter."
　　—Paul Gottfried, editor-in-chief of *Chronicles* and author of
　　After Liberalism: Mass Democracy in the Managerial State

"Bold, lucid, and chilling, *The Total State* takes a flamethrower to every comforting belief conservatives hold about how our political order really works."
　　—Mary Harrington, author of *Feminism Against Progress*

"*The Total State* is a tour de force! MacIntyre exposes the lies of liberalism and socialism alike, and allows us to see how the pseudo-religious myths of individual liberty and collectivism have blinded us to the tyranny which misrules us. At the religious core of this 'total state' is an 'atheistic theocracy' which is really just a parody of Christianity—a powerful parody which can only be defeated by the real thing. Essential reading."
　　—C. C. Pecknold, Professor at The Catholic University
　　of America

"I can't give Auron a greater compliment than he's *the* cultural commentator that has emerged these last few years. I find myself quoting or sharing his thoughts on social media the most often. May his house increase, and may yours as well by reading this book and seriously considering what he has to say."
　　—Steve Deace, BlazeTV host and author of *Rise of the*
　　Fourth Reich

THE TOTAL STATE

THE TOTAL STATE

How Liberal Democracies Become Tyrannies

AURON MACINTYRE

Since 1947
REGNERY

An Imprint of Skyhorse Publishing, Inc.

Regnery books may be purchased in bulk at special discounts for sales promotion, corporate gifts, fund-raising, or educational purposes. Special editions can also be created to specifications. For details, contact the Special Sales Department, Regnery, 307 West 36th Street, 11th Floor, New York, NY 10018 or info@skyhorsepublishing.com.

Regnery® is a registered trademark and its colophon is a trademark of Skyhorse Publishing Inc.®, a Delaware corporation.

Visit our website at www.regnery.com.
Please follow our publisher Tony Lyons on Instagram @tonylyonsisuncertain.

10 9 8 7 6 5 4 3 2

Library of Congress Cataloging-in-Publication Data is available on file.

Cover design by John Caruso
Cover photograph by Shutterstock

Print ISBN: 978-1-68451-558-5
eBook ISBN: 978-1-5107-8155-9

Printed in the United States of America

Dedicated to my loving wife, who kept saying, "You should really write all this down as a book."

And to my parents, who did not just tell me what was worth fighting for, but demonstrated it by how they lived their lives every day.

CONTENTS

And the whole earth was of one language, and of one speech.

And it came to pass, as they journeyed from the east, that they found a plain in the land of Shinar; and they dwelt there.

And they said one to another, Go to, let us make brick, and burn them thoroughly. And they had brick for stone, and slime had they for mortar.

And they said, Go to, let us build us a city and a tower, whose top may reach unto heaven; and let us make us a name, lest we be scattered abroad upon the face of the whole earth.

And the Lord came down to see the city and the tower, which the children of men builded.

And the Lord said, Behold, the people are one, and they have all one language; and this they begin to do: and now nothing will be restrained from them, which they have imagined to do.

Go to, let us go down, and there confound their language, that they may not understand one another's speech.

So the Lord scattered them abroad from thence upon the face of all the earth: and they left off to build the city.

Therefore is the name of it called Babel; because the Lord did there confound the language of all the earth: and from thence did the Lord scatter them abroad upon the face of all the earth.

—The Book of Genesis 11:1–9

INTRODUCTION

I t is very rare to have your entire understanding of how the world works turned upside-down in one year, but that is exactly what happened to me in the summer of 2020.

I had always been fascinated by political and philosophical questions despite not being brought up in a very politically minded household. Twenty-four-hour cable news channels were in their infancy and my parents almost never discussed current events except in passing. But in fourth grade, I received a small personal radio from my grandmother for Christmas, and after listening to some live sports broadcasts on the AM side of the dial, I stumbled upon two men debating politics. I was hooked. The day-to-day churn of the news in the talk radio sphere was entertaining. But as I graduated from grade school and headed off to college to pursue a degree in political science, I discovered that theory was what really sparked my interest. News cycles might drive popular discussion, but political theory showed how the structure of the system drove what happened in day-to-day life.

Unfortunately, there are few jobs available in the field of political theory, so after a brief stint as a history teacher and working as a staffer on a few election campaigns, I found employment as a political reporter for a local newspaper. The stakes were usually pretty low, but seeing the process from the inside changed how I understood politics. Policy and procedure mattered, many great and terrible things were done through their manipulation and mastery, but the media narrative seemed to dominate all other priorities, shaping people's actions in ways I had never thought possible. As a conservative, I'd always known that the press was biased and expected selective coverage and a heavy editorial voice amid what should have been straight news stories. But watching firsthand as journalists completely altered events and details to fit their preselected narratives was eye-opening. My fellow reporters would stand in a press gaggle next to me, hearing the same answers from politicians that I did, and then blatantly manipulate those words, or even fabricate some of their own out of thin air to generate the story they desired. Not only did these people regularly lie, they were actively rewarded for doing so by large progressive news organizations that elevated them for stirring up politically useful controversies.

To take just one example, in 2017, a controversy over removing the statues of Confederate generals culminated in the infamous Unite The Right rally in Charlottesville, Virginia. The national media had already twisted Donald Trump's statement that there "were good people on both sides" of the disagreement over removing Confederate statues. They'd made it sound like he was endorsing the small faction of white nationalists who had marched at the protest. Local reporters were eager to apply the same smear to every Republican imaginable. I was assigned to cover a press conference held by the then-governor of Florida, Rick Scott, who planned to discuss the success of a new jobs program. But one reporter in the press gaggle was determined to write a different story. She badgered the governor, interrupting questions about the jobs program, asking whether Scott agreed with the white nationalists and whether he would denounce President Trump.

Scott was careful not to take the bait. He emphatically condemned the white nationalists while clarifying that Trump's statement had been misrepresented. The journalist was frustrated by Scott's well-crafted answer and insisted on asking the same question in different ways until the governor forgot to repeat his denouncement of the white nationalists while defending Trump. The journalist immediately pounced on this isolated clip, writing a headline that accused Scott of being sympathetic to the white nationalists. The headline was a lie, but it was the story the press wanted, and it was reported widely. The Florida journalist who had manufactured the lie was soon promoted to a national outlet.

The Donald Trump candidacy and later presidency seemed to magnify all the worst impulses of the press. Liberal journalists hated Trump and red-state Americans so much that it seemed to drive them to derangement. Even in my relatively low-pressure local news environment, most reporters treated every story that might relate to national politics as an opportunity to strike a blow against the New York real estate tycoon. No shadowy cabal of overlords was handing down marching orders; no editorial meeting was held confirming an anti-Trump direction; but every low-level propagandist with a journalism degree suddenly thought it was their solemn duty to destroy the orange menace. No falsehood was too great, and any and every distortion of the truth could be justified in the name of damaging what these zealots saw as the second coming of Adolf Hitler.

Watching the dedication that even inconsequential journalists brought to this jihad against Trump had me questioning my own preconceived notions about power. In the beginning, I had no personal feelings about the man. During the Republican primary, he proved to be charismatic, but he was also crass and his grasp on policy seemed narrow. I assumed he would be a flashy but shallow celebrity candidate who would make a few headlines before burning out. But as he started to pull away from the pack, it became clear Trump was willing to address issues like trade and immigration that were incredibly important to the Republican base but had been largely ignored by the establishment. Most importantly, Trump was willing to attack the media for their obvious bias. The base knew something instinctively that I had only begun to grasp. The press, and the ruling class they represented, despised middle America and were happy to exploit and destroy what they saw as backward hicks for fun and profit. Hillary Clinton would later confirm this with her infamous "basket of deplorables" comment about Trump supporters.

Experts of every stripe seemed willing to humiliate themselves to stop the election of Donald Trump. Psychiatrists appeared on television to diagnose him with a slate of dangerous psychological conditions and authoritarian personality traits. Reporters lied on air relentlessly, deceptively editing audio and video with no regard for the damage it might do to their long-term credibility. Newscasters attacked Trump with accusations of "dog-whistle racism," slandered his voters with charges of racial identitarianism, and even denied the existence of critical race theory, a controversial educational doctrine that had many parents concerned about what their children were learning in public schools. Even election pollsters, whose livelihoods are theoretically based on their ability to accurately predict election results without bias, gave Hillary Clinton a ridiculous 99 percent chance to defeat Trump. The readiness of trusted institutions to debase themselves was almost cartoonish, yet Trump secured an Electoral College victory and became the forty-fifth president of the United States.

The treatment of Trump during his campaign and subsequent presidency caused me to ask some critical questions. In previous decades, most Americans had favored immigration restrictions, economic protectionism, aggressive policing, and a restrained foreign policy. If the democratic political process was about responding to public opinion, why was it impossible to get candidates to run on these almost universally favored positions? Why did the GOP, a party that claimed to care about families, support economic policies that destroyed family formation and stability? Why did the Democrats, a party that claimed to care about stopping war and the military industrial complex, suddenly lean into military intervention the minute Donald Trump announced his general aversion to war? I looked for answers to these questions outside the talk radio and cable news echo chamber, but came away frustrated, still locked in the frame of mind that the media and my own schooling had instilled in me. It would take a black swan event of the most epic proportions to shake me out of my slumber.

When the COVID pandemic arrived in 2020, things happened slowly and then all at once. A virus causing havoc in China was all over the news, but experts like a then-unknown doctor by the name of Anthony Fauci were telling the public there was nothing to fear. The main concern of politicians seemed to be that fears over the virus would cause racism. Democrat Nancy Pelosi joined up with local politicians and encouraged shoppers to continue patronizing businesses in San Francisco's Chinatown. Residents were told to hug an Asian person on the street to show how silly it was to fear the virus.

Then, suddenly, the virus was reported across every continent. Scenes of overpacked hospitals in nations like Italy panicked politicians and the number of cases in America spiked. Officials cancelled large gatherings while closing parks, beaches, and schools. Businesses sent their employees home and churches were forced to close their doors. No legislation had been passed, no war had been declared, but most of the population suddenly found themselves locked in their homes. Big box retailers were allowed to continue operating due to their status as the primary food distribution hubs in many areas, but only small numbers of patrons could visit at any one time and they had to wear face masks. City streets were empty, with many municipalities requiring special permits that designated an individual as an "essential worker" to be on the road. Civilization had ground to a halt.

At first, most complied with the lockdowns out of fear. The fog of war had made it difficult to know how dangerous the virus really was, and if the apocalypse had truly come it seemed best to play it safe. But as "fourteen days to slow the spread" turned into months of house arrest, many grew skeptical. The virus was certainly real—hundreds of thousands Americans would die from it—but COVID-19 mostly affected the elderly and many healthy young people did not want to be held hostage. At that time, no vaccine existed and no one knew how long it would be before scientists were able to develop one and produce it for mass consumption. Americans did not want to live like this forever. A large percentage of the population was ready to get back to normal and take whatever risks might come.

The experts who had locked down the entire country were drunk on the incredible power they had amassed in the space of only a few months and had no interest in letting it go. Many state and local governments worked in concert with federal agencies to treat those who opposed the lockdowns as the equivalent of public-health terrorists. Business owners who attempted to

xvi   *The Total State*

open shop were fined millions of dollars, parents who took their children to the park were threatened, and pastors who attempted to hold church services were arrested. One pastor, Rodney Howard-Browne, was arrested for "reckless disregard for human life" after attempting to gather with his congregation in Tampa, Florida. The owner of Atilis Gym in New Jersey racked up over sixty citations, carrying $1.2 million in fines for refusing to close his doors during the pandemic. Little to no action was taken to challenge the constitutionality of these restrictions and punishments.

I was absolutely blown away by what had unfolded before me. The US Constitution was the bedrock of my American identity. I had been told all my life that the carefully crafted checks and balances built into the system limited the government's ability to seize power in exactly this manner. Even if all the branches of government were to work in unison to encroach on people's freedom, the Bill of Rights stood as a final bulwark against the destruction of our liberties. I had been told the Second Amendment existed primarily to make sure nothing like this could ever happen. Yet freedom of assembly and worship had been summarily abolished and very few people seemed to care. Obviously the politicians had buckled under but even those around me who I'd known for decades and who largely shared my political views were happy to go along. Conservatives and libertarians who had spent their whole lives railing against government tyranny found ways to excuse and deflect. When tyranny came, nothing happened. The

Constitution I'd believed in my whole life did nothing. Those who had parroted the myth of limited government seemed to go on as if nothing important had been lost.

That summer, lockdowns eventually gave way to riots. The death of George Floyd unleashed a wave of violence across the nation. Those who had shuttered their churches and businesses watched them turn to ash in a racial conflagration, cheered on by their political and cultural leaders. Corporations sponsored the violence by contributing to funds that bailed out the rioters and scientists manufactured obvious lies to explain why racism was a public health crisis and rioting actually reduced the spread of the virus. The pandemic was then used to justify a transformation of the voting system through mass mail-in ballots, which helped remove Donald Trump from the White House. The final strands of my faith in the system had been severed. Everything I had been taught about how politics and government worked, and had repeated in a professional capacity, was a lie. I needed to understand why. I needed the truth.

So I turned to a new set of thinkers, those well outside the mainstream, those no high school teacher, college professor, or conservative commentator had ever mentioned to me. These political theorists and moral philosophers forced me to reevaluate the founding narrative of our current regime. That narrative goes something like this:

For most of history, man toiled under all-powerful kings, tyrants who wielded total control. Their every word was law. Religion, tradition, and obligation combined to create a system that crippled science, innovation, and progress. Then, in the 1600s, philosophers took up the tools of skepticism and reason from the burgeoning discipline of science and began applying them to politics. Discarding the stifling assumptions of the past, these thinkers developed more rational foundations for the state, revivifying an ancient form of government, the democratic republic, that would come to dominate the Western world. Democracy would give the people, not some parasitic aristocracy, power. Through voting, citizens would elect a government of their choosing, granting it sovereignty only if it agreed to protect the rights of the people.

Separation of powers and a carefully crafted system of checks and balances would combine with elections to safeguard against the expansion of government. Limited government would guarantee the individual unprecedented levels of liberty, which would unleash the creative energies and productivity of mankind. This new form of social organization would require a few revolutions to get started, first in America, then in France, but as the massive advantages of liberal democracy became clear, countries would begin to make more peaceful transitions. The age of reason and science was yielding unprecedented progress and abundance, and anyone who wanted to compete in the new world would be wise to follow the democratic trend.

Anyone who has sat in an American classroom is familiar with this narrative. It forms the core ideology of the political Right in the United States, and even the Left will repeat it now and then, while adding the caveat that the promise of freedom has never been truly recognized due to systemic racism and the oppression of women. Freedom won; tyranny lost. We all live lives of unprecedented liberty and prosperity under a government limited by constitutional principles and constrained by the will of the people . . . or do we?

What if the nature of human beings didn't magically change during the fabled period we call the Enlightenment? What if the nature of political power and the desire of leaders to acquire it were never altered by science or reason? What if the story our leaders have repeated endlessly about liberal democracy and popular sovereignty has actually served to expand the power of the state to unprecedented levels, all while assuring the ruled that they live in an era of freedom unlike any that's ever been experienced?

With the swift implementation of emergency government power during the COVID pandemic and increasing pressure from institutions both public and private to enforce the speech code we call political correctness, it is not uncommon for the average person to feel like freedom is under attack. Many, especially on the right, express dissatisfaction over this arrangement, but the problem is always treated as temporary or recent. The pandemic was a sudden and unexpected health crisis threatening the lives of millions, yes, and uncomfortable liberties were taken with government power. But it was all with the intention of protecting public health.

Whatever restrictions were put in place, they will by definition be temporary. Eventually the virus will subside and the freedoms we previously enjoyed will be restored. Political correctness, while it does restrict freedom of speech, is a cultural movement primarily enforced by private entities like employers, the media, and public intellectuals. It's the result of a weak, pampered generation of college students who will grow out of their hypersensitivity once they enter the real world and have to endure actual hardships.

It never seems to occur to those who spout these platitudes that the developments they identify are neither recent nor sudden, that they are the predictable result of a process that has been ongoing for generations. The water in the pot has been growing hotter for decades, but only recently have the frogs noticed it is boiling. Yet all this is treated as an unfortunate slowdown on the inevitable march toward ever-greater liberty. Every culture has setbacks, rough patches, and unforeseen emergencies, but in the end, the government as it was constructed by the founding fathers will protect us and ensure we return to the path we were on.

Those who cannot express the mildest opinion in public, who cannot raise their children in their own values (or, in many cases, afford to have children at all), see themselves as ambassadors of freedom to the world. Those who can be forced to wear a mask, have their businesses and churches shut down, and be functionally trapped in their homes while groups favored by the ruling class are allowed to burn and loot cities, still cling to the narrative of ever-increasing liberty. Even those who are gravely concerned by the actions of their government, and the passivity with which their fellow citizens seem to accept them, still see this as a subversion, not a consequence, of the system into which they were born.

If we are to understand what is happening around us, we need to be willing to ask ourselves an uncomfortable question. What if the story we have been told, and have probably told ourselves many times over, is not true?

In *The Republic*, Plato introduced the concept of the noble lie, a falsehood told by the leaders of the state to the common people in order to make it easier to accept their rule, to lend it legitimacy in the eyes of its subjects. Like it or not, every country has some version of this. But there are noble lies that hew closely to the truth with some embellishment that passes into myth as time goes by, and there are noble lies that are a complete obfuscation of the way the state functions. If we have been told all our lives that we live in an age of unprecedented liberty protected by constitutional limits on government and individual rights, but find a government that is ever-expanding, extending its tentacles into areas previously never thought imaginable, then we must be willing to consider that we were sold a falsehood.

What does it mean if the Constitution does not meaningfully restrain government power? How do we approach politics if power itself does not seem to conform to the rules we have been taught since we were young? Why has liberal democracy, a system built on the principles of freedom and popular sovereignty, yielded a level of control that the most tyrannical kings of old could only dream of?

This book will attempt to answer these questions. It will explain the nature of the total state, why a liberal and free society would produce one, and how power actually functions in our government. By better understanding what brought us to this point and why, we can better assess what, if anything, can be done about it. I won't pretend answers are easy or obvious—far from it—but without a clear understanding of how we got here and where here is, any attempt to save our country is doomed.

CHAPTER 1

The Nature of the Total State

In the beginning, all states were total. The earliest civilizations were small. A few families would band together to form an extended clan and establish a village. Generally, one male became dominant, named chieftain either through the right of combat or by demonstrating the ability to provide—usually a mixture of both. In a small village or nomadic tribe, everyone needed to do their jobs. Most people were farmers or hunters, and while some hunters might have developed special skills such as in the art of making weapons, there simply wasn't enough efficiency or redundancy in any one area to carry those who did not contribute to the immediate survival of the clan. Relatives could feed you and take care of you for a few days if you injured yourself or got sick. But no one could become a professional author or painter or scientist because everyone's efforts had to be devoted to preservation.

Since everyone is key to the survival of the state, the state must take an interest in everyone. If someone refused to plant, hunt, harvest, cook, or fight outsiders, this had an immediate impact on the well-being of the whole group and the offender would find himself punished or ostracized. No chieftain could expect his clan to last long if it was full of lazy cowards. A small civilization would have to enforce penalties for such behavior if it was to thrive and grow.

If the clan did grow, it might build a network of villages. It might gather enough surplus under the guidance of its ruler to allow some to specialize in different skills, technologies, and other advantages that would benefit the whole society. The freedom to specialize would accelerate development. The additional surplus and safety the civilization gained would allow its people to take on occupations that did not immediately translate into food or martial power. If a system of mutual exchange was established, such occupations could then trade what they produced for the products of the farmer or hunter. The chieftain, now closer to what we would call a king, no longer needed to be interested in every individual. Indoctrination and positive reinforcement through tradition and social institutions would generate enough prosocial behavior to keep things going in the right direction amid an increasingly hands-off approach.

Modern man is born into a society that is much farther down this road. Our civilization has so much built-in efficiency, redundancy, and stability that a large segment of the populace no longer needs to work in roles essential to survival. This, in large part, helps to generate the feeling of freedom so many associate with the modern world. When the individual does not need to work very hard to purchase his food, and security is more or less a given, it creates a lot more free time and takes the pressure off when it comes to career choices. The bad news is that most of us will squander that time and opportunity, but some will design new rocket ships, so it ends up being a net positive, right?

In a society of abundance and security, we begin to feel entitled to choice and leisure, which comes at little to no cost. The days of constant oversight are far in the rear-view mirror, with even the discipline and prosocial behavior that tradition and institutions used to instill discarded as unnecessary and stifling. This is about as far away from the total state as you can get.

For America, this apex came in the 1990s, and to those born in that era, it seemed like the natural order of things. Pax Americana had been in place for decades. An attack on the homeland was unthinkable. Liberal democracy had conquered the world and brought unprecedented prosperity to all. No one in America would go hungry. The ancient clash of religions seemed to have given way to a detente of plurality, of live and let live. The internet was an infinite source of wealth and possibility. Soon everyone would go to college and get a nice big salary working an email job at a tech company. The ugly work of manual production and security could be outsourced to others. The major problems of civilization had been solved. Some even wrote books saying this was the end of political history.

Most of those celebrating did not, however, address the fact that the triumph of liberal democracy had its own implications for the way the state interacted with its people. Under what we think of as a more traditional form of government, like a monarchy, the will of the people does matter, but it is not the mandate on which authority rests. The king must always avoid becoming so tyrannical that he inspires a popular uprising, but the people being temporarily dissatisfied is not usually a direct challenge to his power. The king is not the king because the people select him every few years. In a democracy, however, the rulers are, at least theoretically, legitimated by popular sovereignty.

We are taught this is what holds the ruling class accountable: they must listen to and obey the will of the people or lose the power they so dearly covet. Yet this is not how the relationship really works. There's a reason the incumbency rate for members of Congress reliably hovers around 90 percent while Congress's popularity remains mired in the single digits. If the will of the people is the key to legitimating the power of the ruling class, then the ruling class must take an interest in controlling the will of the people. The good news for our elite is that mass media provides the perfect tool for doing this.

As true mass media was born, good liberals like Walter Lippman were kind enough to write books explaining why it was the duty of elites to use this new tool to steer the will of the people in the right direction for the common good. The ruling class thus became deeply involved in controlling the information the public receives and the narrative that information shapes. Most high schoolers get a brief lesson in how yellow journalism impacted the Spanish-American War and then pretend such malpractice is a thing of the past. But, of course, it isn't.

Still, while large-scale information manipulation is required for leaders in a democracy to keep power, it does not, in and of itself, lead to the total state. When newspapers had a monopoly on information distribution, they could be relied on to deliver a plurality of voters armed with the correct opinion. You didn't have to fool all the people all the time, just meet a threshold high enough to maintain power. This meant the government did not have to seek total hegemony. It was the internet that changed this in a dramatic way.

In an essay on the total state, political theorist Curtis Yarvin points out that in the modern age, the internet has fundamentally transformed how information flows and therefore the government's relationship with its people. The explosion of alternative news sites, amateur video journalism, and podcasts have damaged the monolithic narrative the media was once able to deliver. Though the majority still have their worldview shaped by mainstream sources and probably will for the foreseeable future, the real game-changer is social media.

In a democracy, power is never secure, always up for grabs, with the next struggle only one news cycle away. Social media gives everyone a platform and therefore turns everyone into a combatant. Anyone can go viral at a moment's notice with an outraged Facebook post, a passionate video, or a funny meme. The political opinions of average people can reach millions in a way that was once only possible for media barons and their handpicked journalists and columnists. This is a huge problem for those who have carefully cultivated power. When dissident opinions were shared privately between friends, or even shouted on a street corner, they could be largely ignored. Such upstarts didn't have enough reach and could easily be dismissed as cranks. When the same opinions were printed on a pamphlet, that might be a little more concerning, but they could still be drowned out by the firehose of propaganda the elite could turn on the public through the mainstream press.

With every citizen able to instantaneously communicate his opinions on a mass scale, the threat posed to elites who rely on popular sovereignty for power was substantial. New methods had to be deployed. This is why political opinions are now routinely censored by social media companies, though this is actually the least effective method of censorship because it is so obvious. Direct exercises of power tend to bring attention to those responsible for them, and people take notice. The elite would like to avoid engaging in obvious censorship, as it gives up the game, so more subtle methods are preferred.

The threat of losing one's job or social standing is a far more powerful weapon. Sure, you might go viral in your video denouncing the government, but the media will proclaim you a bigot in front of tens of millions of people and you will be out of work by the end of the day. You'll be lucky if you're still married and your friends are still talking to you by the end of the week. Even the rich and powerful are not immune. In 2014, Mozilla CEO and co-founder Brendan Eich was forced to step down from his position when it was discovered he had donated $1,000 to support Proposition 8, a 2008 measure that would have banned gay marriage in California. Even the vague threat of controversy was enough for the tech company to cancel one of its founders.

This is why so many opinions and even criticisms tend to be safe and sterilized. The powerful do not ban all dissent—that would be foolish and human nature will buck against it every time. Instead they allow only ineffective criticism as a blow-off valve to release pressure within the system while ensuring they are never really threatened.

As we approach the total state, however, a more sinister form of narrative manipulation rears its head. When everyone has a platform, they are not only able to share their political views, they are expected to. Important things are happening. We are in a struggle for the future of this nation and because it is a democracy every vote counts. You don't want to seem shallow and selfish, do you? When everyone has a megaphone at their fingertips, it is not only the passionate political pronouncements but the lack thereof that draws attention.

As Yarvin puts it, "In a total state, everyone and everything is infused with power. Everyone matters. Everything is important. Everyone has to care. Everyone wants to change the world. Everyone must be engaged. Everyone is pushing power forward, or pushing back against it. Everyone is either a collaborator or a dissident. Power has turned the whole country into a political

cult."[1] And since the only form of acceptable pronounce-
ment in such a cult is to support those in power, one
must not only avoid looking suspicious, one must post
correctly.

While technology previously allowed governments
to move away from the total state by facilitating specialization, efficiency, redundancy, and surplus, with
the dominance of democracy and social media, the
total state has made its return. While we are told that
we live in one of the freest societies in history, people
feel compelled not only to limit what they say online,
but to parrot the political opinions of their teachers,
bosses, and peers lest they be singled out for their
silence. Early on, the threat of a viral video revealing
your unorthodox political opinion might have kept you
silent, but now failing to loudly signal compliance with
your social media posts can be damning. The modern citizen lives in a panopticon of coworkers, family,
friends, and superiors. Each is constantly attempting
to ensure not only that no wrongthink is ever publicly
expressed, but that a sufficient stream of rightthink is
dutifully posted.

Major universities are increasingly moving away
from standardized tests as their main tool of admissions
selection in favor of personal essays and résumés with
a heavy emphasis on community involvement. This is
a thinly veiled shift toward political loyalty as the key

---

1   Yarvin, Curtis. "A general theory of collaboration." https://gray
     mirror.substack.com/p/1-a-general-theory-of-collaboration

decider for admittance. The sentiments expressed in the personal essay, the topics chosen for emphasis, and the organizations chosen for participation provide a pretty clear picture of what political priors the student will bring. University education has become the portal through which almost everyone who enters the elite must pass—which means the vast majority of those who rule in the future will have been chosen on the basis of ideology, not merit.

This brings up an obvious question: One can see why those in charge need to manipulate public opinion to stay in power, but how do they coordinate the message? The United States does not have a king or an official ruling party, so how does the elite decide what people should think and how to make them think it? In the kind of totalitarian state we have been conditioned to recognize, there are officials and even entire government divisions with this job. The Nazis had Joseph Goebbels; the Soviets had the Politburo. Whether the title was official or not, everyone understood who was crafting the narrative and that they did so with the authority of the state.

Yarvin uses the story of the German cat to help us understand what is taking place today. In the 1930s, there was a Jewish reporter living in Germany who had a subscription to a cat magazine. The magazine featured the kinds of articles you would expect: pieces about raising your cat, grooming your cat, what toys are best for your cat. Yet as the 1930s wore on, the magazine began to feature articles about "the German Cat" and its superior loyalty and character. Eventually, it came to be dominated by such pieces.

The point is that in the total state, no media is ever truly about its stated topic but is rather an opportunity to further state propaganda. The dissemination of the narrative becomes the primary goal of each and every media outlet.

For anyone living in our current society, this should sound eerily familiar. Movies, novels, and even comic books are rife with political messaging. Political allegory and satire have always had their place in storytelling, but they have since come to dominate everything. Even children's books are full of political propaganda. Roald Dahl, the author of many beloved children's novels like *Charlie and the Chocolate Factory*, has seen his work posthumously edited to remove "offensive terminology" and insert new politically correct phrases. Sporting events and hobbies that were once famously apolitical, that served to bring together a divided culture, have become dominated by displays of political fealty by athletes who style themselves as activists.

Again, this raises the question: If there is no official state organ coordinating the message, no Goebbels pushing this from the top down, then why is the German cat appearing everywhere?

For Yarvin, the answer is a decentralized network of organizations and individuals responsible for manufacturing a cultural consensus that he calls the Cathedral. To be clear, the Cathedral is not some conspiracy of Illuminati members. Yarvin does not believe such a conspiracy exists. What he means are those players responsible for crafting and popularizing ideas, mainly the news and entertainment media, the public education system, the permanent bureaucracy inside the federal government, and, most importantly, the universities. These are the entities from which most of the ideas that make their way into the public consciousness originate and they arrive at similar conclusions on a shockingly regular basis. This is the Cathedral at work.

Think about a handful of our most elite institutions: Harvard, Yale, the *New York Times*, and the *Washington Post*. We've been told we live in a marketplace of ideas, an intellectual Darwinian arena where theories compete and only the strong survive. Harvard, then, should be competing with Yale and the *Times* competing with the *Post*. They should be locked in an ongoing and brutal war for intellectual supremacy— but how often do they actually disagree? The answer is almost never. Video compilations of dozens of news anchors all saying exactly the same thing word for word have become very popular on social media. It is enough to make the average person ask whether these organizations are in competition at all.

It is not just that media organizations and universities seem to agree with their alleged competition the vast majority of the time; it is that all other organizations in the business of manufacturing consensus also seem to agree. When Harvard comes to a conclusion on an issue of public policy, Yale is soon to follow, the media quickly reports the findings, government bureaucracy implements them, and schools are teaching them in short order. There is almost never any serious public debate over these issues, and if there is any pushback from the plebs, the media knows to smear them as ignorant racists until they back down. Once the experts have spoken, there is nothing left to do but inform the public of their dictates and begin their implementation. Again, this requires a high degree of message coordination and implementation without a formal organization getting it done, and that has to be explained.

Yarvin does so through the concept of the meme. In the popular consciousness, the meme is a funny picture with some words attached, but the term actually has its origins in the field of evolutionary biology. Before Richard Dawkins became popular for making childishly simple and embarrassing arguments against Christianity, he was well known in the scientific community for inventing the concept of the meme. Dawkins wanted to explain how something like religion, which often demands actions that are not evolutionarily advantageous to the individual like martyrdom, could be so prevalent throughout human history.

Dawkins' big breakthrough was to explain that ideas could act like viruses of the mind, could take on evolutionary lives of their own. The religious idea does not care about the well-being of its host so long as it is able to reproduce and spread. In this way, ideas can infect entire civilizations and basically hijack them for their own purposes. This might be an incredibly crude way to explain how a religion functions, but it does help the modern secular mind grasp how and why individuals and entire cultures can form themselves around a set of ideas.

(Now, if only Dawkins had considered that he could fall prey to the same phenomenon.)

As modern Westerners born into a scientific age, we tend to think of religion in very specific terms. Religions have holy books, one or more supernatural deities, places of worship, and sacred symbols. If a belief system doesn't have these key attributes, we tend not to identify it as religious. But this is a mistake. Dawkins and millions of people like him have beliefs that inform their worldview, their goals, and their actions. These beliefs can be loosely identified as progressive liberalism. Dawkins would no doubt balk at the idea, but in practice, progressive liberalism informs his actions in the same way that Islam informs the actions of its adherents. Both Dawkins and the Muslim are committed to the practice of their faith.

This is how the Cathedral serves as a coordination mechanism between so many different organizations in our society: it provides them with the same religious values. Anyone who is going to serve as a leader at the State Department, a reporter at a television station, an opinion editor at a newspaper, or a teacher at a public school has to spend four to eight years in the same place: the university system. They do so during a formative time in their lives when everyone who holds the keys to their future believes in the same moral system: progressive liberalism. Whatever religion these students may check on their admissions forms, progressivism will be what they swim in while they're at college. Learning its tenets, repeating them accurately, and practicing them carefully will be the key to success while they are earning their degrees. Climbing the professional hierarchy will be dependent on navigating the progressive code.

Everyone in power will thus have attended similar educational institutions and obtained their positions in a similar way. In a deeply Christian community, there was no need to ask what code of ethics was being applied in any given situation, what rules would inform the decisions being made. No one was required to state out loud that Christianity was the foundation of the society and that it dictated the terms of almost every decision. It was implicitly understood. The university serves as the modern church. No conspiracy is required to coordinate the actions of those who manufacture the narrative of our civilization because they all go to the same house of worship. They are all singing from the same hymn sheet.

Progressivism, like any morality based on religious principles, is self-policing. If a journalist, professor, or bureaucrat decides to step out of line, their colleagues will quickly chastise them back into line. If they do not show sufficient deference to the ruling morality, their professional advancement will cease and they will be ostracized from polite company. If the infraction is severe enough, the entire weight of the ruling class can crush the heretic in public, branding them a bigot, racist, or fascist. Ideas tend to flow from the university down to the lower strata of the cathedral. Because the network is decentralized, adoption can sometimes be slow or piece-meal, but eventually everyone learns to get onboard or face the consequences.

As odd as it sounds, we are governed by a decentralized atheistic theocracy. A religious system without an official holy book or central church, but a religious system of moral assumptions all the same. It is particularly difficult for Americans to perceive this due to our understanding of the public/private distinction. We are trained to think that formal power, officially centralized under the law by the government, is the only path to tyranny. If power is distributed among non-state actors, it is thus difficult for Americans to see it as a threat. This is understandable as the founding fathers never envisioned a secular society where the entire ruling class received moral instruction exclusively from progressive universities before taking jobs that allowed them to deliver a narrative to a small box in every American's pocket 24/7, but this is the world we live in.

During the riot at the Capitol building on January 6, 2021, a can of Axe body spray that had been left on the ground appeared in a photograph circulated on social media. The company felt compelled to denounce the protests publicly as if having their product on-site would be seen as an act of disobedience by those in power. During the Black Lives Matter riots in 2020, too many companies to name publicly endorsed the cause of the rioters without hesitation and without needing to be encouraged. Even noticing that the destruction was severe and was going unpunished sent too much of a signal to those in power whom the corporations wanted to ingratiate themselves with.

M&Ms, the candy brand, announced in 2022 they would "diversify" their line of cartoon mascots. Those mascots have no racial characteristics—they're giant talking M&Ms—but that hardly mattered. What mattered was that M&Ms said the right thing. The National Basketball Association, National Football League, and NASCAR have all signaled similiar allegiance to the diversity, equity, and inclusion cause by donating tens of millions of dollars to associated groups. In the total state, no one needs to tell corporations what is expected of them; it is understood as morally necessary.

We now have a definition of the total state and an understanding of how it coordinates despite lacking an official central propaganda organ. Next we will explore another confusing aspect of our march toward the total state and why so few of us noticed its advance.

CHAPTER 2

Social Spheres and the Expansion of the State

As we analyze the total state, a few obvious questions emerge. If the power of the state has expanded to unprecedented levels, why does the average person believe they live in an age of unprecedented freedom and liberal democracy? If the system around us is growing ever more totalitarian, should that not be obvious to everyone?

Much of the confusion comes from a misunderstanding about how much power has been wielded by other forms of government throughout history. We are taught that monarchs were more or less omnipotent, that their word was law, and that they could command anything at a whim, but this was far from the case. A king certainly held great authority, but in most cases he was simply the first among nobles rather than some kind of god-emperor. This was especially true in the West. A king required the buy-in of other members of the aristocracy to rule. He needed to call on his barons for both military power and social influence while also depending on them to collect the taxes he needed to keep the state going.

This inability of the king to manage the realm on his own required him to grant great autonomy to those nobles. The regional barons were the ones who regularly interacted with the average citizen, helped to solve their disputes, and provided them with protection. The loyalty of the peasant belonged first to his regional lord, with the king managing a domain that was essentially a patchwork of local political networks. Far from wielding supreme power, the king often had to negotiate with his barons, offering them personal or political favors in exchange for troops in the next military campaign or gold from the treasury. Many today would see this as corruption, but the necessity for regional political patronage kept the monarch from growing too powerful.

The nobility was just one center of power that the king had to navigate. The Catholic Church was the religious, cultural, and social center for many European societies. It exerted great influence over the morals and values of the people and a ruler ignored it at their own peril. Merchant guilds, civic fraternities, and other social organizations also demanded loyalty, binding the people into blocks of constituencies that had to be negotiated with at one level or another in order to rule. Far from being autonomous, the individual was a member of a family, clan, church, guild, and barony, each with its own obligations and protections that had to be respected.

In his book *On Power,* Bertrand de Jouvenel explains that it is the collapse of these competing social spheres that has allowed government to centralize and grow more totalitarian while making the individual feel more liberated. Historically, a large extended family was the norm, binding together children, parents, siblings, uncles, aunts, and cousins. Churches and other community organizations lent aid, but care for an ailing grandparent or destitute niece fell primarily on the family.

As the bonds that held together traditional societies wore away, the obligations that foundational communal institutions had once placed on the individual faded. Families shrank, church attendance fell, unions and civic organizations dissolved, and the individual was suddenly freed from these obligations. Even his residual duties, like caring for an ailing or destitute loved one, were largely transferred to the state. Insurance for the unemployed, medical care, social security, the supervision and education of children, all that used to burden the individual was lifted off of his shoulders. This is how a totalizing government has made unprecedented demands on its subjects without them feeling the squeeze. It replaced the competing social spheres that had previously served to check the power of the state and removed the extensive personal commitments they had entailed.

"Why is it not clear as crystal to everyone that the private citizen is falling ever more deeply into the public authority's debt for those commodities?" de Jouvenal wrote. "And what is the explanation of the fact that, right down to our own time, the movement of history has in general been interpreted as a progressive liberation of the individual? The reason is that there are in society in addition to the state and the individual, social authorities as well, which also claim from the human being their due of obedience and services. And the diminution or disappearance of his obligations to a social authority may affect his life and stir his interest more than the aggravation of his obligations to the political authority."[1]

The modern state collects more in taxes than most regimes in history ever have. It can demand the mass conscription of military-aged males into its armed forces, a power most kings could not have dreamed of. Technology allows the modern state to monitor and censor the speech of its subjects to a degree unimaginable to the most tyrannical dictators of the past. Yet so long as this is done while freeing the individual from traditional social obligations, not only do its citizens not feel oppressed, they see themselves as liberated.

This narrative is also assisted by the myth of government progressing from the hierarchy of nobility to the equality of popular sovereignty. A liberal democracy rules in the name of the people, and in theory, the government speaks with the voice of the citizenry and acts with their authority. If the state is working to secure and protect the liberty of the people, almost anything can be demanded in their name. What is so sacred that it cannot be sacrificed for the rights of the masses? Now that

---

1   Bertrand De Jouvenel, *On Power*, p.172.

the competing spheres of social control have collapsed, what is there to protect against the designs of such a government?

Much of the twentieth century was framed as a battle between two competing political ideologies, liberal democracy versus communism, individual rights on one side and collectivism on the other. But de Jouvenel asserted that the two political systems had the same end goal: the total state. Those in charge naturally look for ways to increase their power, centralizing all duties and loyalties to themselves. This can be done by casting themselves as liberators, freeing the people from the yoke of obligation to their regional powers, or, in the case of competing social spheres, the duty of caring for one's family or of attending church. A communist regime can also offer liberation from the capitalist class, the competing economic sphere portrayed as a parasite upon the freedom and wellbeing of the worker.

Under both the liberal and communist archetypes, the functions that these competing institutions once served are transferred to state-managed bureaucracies. Theoretically, these neutral civil servants manage the delivery of highly efficient services without the patronage and agendas prevalent in a regional aristocracy. In reality, this means the civil servants are completely dependent on the state for their power and status. A "neutral" civil service exam may be instituted to give the impression of selection by objective merit, but a matrix of exceptions and preferences, like affirmative action, can slowly be added to mold the bureaucracy until its loyalty can be assured. The system of bureaucracy thus enables the centralization of power and loyalty by allowing the ruler to manage an ever-larger domain without the need to negotiate with competing political spheres.

Because no ruler exists in a vacuum, they must always be aware of the power competing states wield and the degree of control they have over their populaces. If a neighboring country acquires the power of mass conscription over its citizens, leaders will eventually seek to utilize it to their advantage. States must, at minimum, demonstrate the capacity to make a similar demand of their citizens or risk being destroyed by their neighbors. This is how totalitarian state power becomes an arms race. No nation dares to fall behind when it comes to control of their subjects, lest it lead to their destruction or annexation.

By dissolving the bonds and obligations of family, tribe, and religion, the ruler can make his subjects entirely loyal to and dependent on the state. Liberalism does this in the name of freedom for the individual, while socialism does it in the name of the collective good, but the result is the same.

"Where will it end?" inquires de Jouvenel. "In the destruction of all other command for the benefit of one alone—that of the state. In each man's absolute freedom from every family and social authority, a freedom the price of which is complete submission to the state. In the complete equality as between themselves of all citizens, paid for by their equal abasement before the power of their absolute master—the state. In the disappearance of every constraint which does not emanate from the state, and in the denial of every pre-eminence which is not approved by the state. In a word, it ends in the atomization of society, and in the rupture of every private tie linking man and man, whose only bond is now their common bondage to the state. The extremes of individualism and socialism meet: that was their predestined course."[2]

We can see the erosion of those final competing bonds in the contemporary application of sexual identities to children. Immediate family is the hardest sphere of social influence for the total state to eliminate. In previous societies, memberships in churches, professional guilds, and community organizations were, more or less, functions of birth. The expansion of state power in the name of individual liberty has made these affiliations voluntary, which has decimated their membership and collapsed their power. But family is a much tougher nut to crack. Most people are born into some sort of family and are therefore unavoidably bound up in its identity and obligations.

Meaningful attempts have been made by the government to prevent these bonds from ever forming in the first place by subsidizing single motherhood, for example. In many cases, this has made it costlier, both in terms of money and independence, for mothers to marry the fathers of their children. This has helped to devastate family formation in lower-income communities, and the trend has since traveled up the socioeconomic ladder as

---

2   Bertrand de Jouvenel, *On Power*, p.187.

well. But even a broken family can serve as a sphere of competing loyalty, and so the total emancipation of the child from the authority of their parents is required.

There is a reason why every organ of power in the United States seems obsessed with introducing sexual and gender identity to children at an increasingly young age. Normalizing the idea of transexual children is an incredibly useful tool for the regime because it can serve as a reliable wedge between kids and their parents. If children can choose their own gender, if the ability to choose their gender is a human right, then it becomes the duty of the government to protect that right. Protect that right from whom, you might ask? The parents, of course.

Any sane parent knows you cannot let seven-year-olds define their own reality. Children still believe monsters live under the bed. They think if they run off the edge of the roof fast enough, they might be able to fly. It is the duty of parents as caretakers to provide them with a well-adjusted and healthy view of themselves and the world around them. This duty gives parents authority, an authority that creates loyalty which then competes with the state.

If children are taught at a young age that gender is something they can choose, then they will experiment with it. A parent who corrects their child's understanding will be considered in violation of their rights, giving the state the opportunity to intervene. According to trans ideology, children have the human right to choose their gender independent of their parents, but of course no seven-year-old is truly autonomous. Every child is dependent on their parents and in ways far deeper than just material need. Anyone who is arguing for the autonomy of the child is actually arguing for the state to assume authority over the child.

This is why the logic of individual autonomy is so useful to state expansion. No man is an island unto himself. No matter how much we like to perceive ourselves as totally independent, we all have social, spiritual, and physical needs that can only be met by communities of our fellow man. At every turn, the state must thus offer to liberate the naive individual by taking onto itself the responsibilities once held by the organic communities that placed demands on him. This is always a devil's bargain, however, as we never actually escape dependence or duty; we simply transfer it to the state.

The government's response to the COVID-19 pandemic is an instructive example of this. The entire ordeal perfectly demonstrates how quickly the illusion of individual rights and limited government that modern liberal democracies have constructed can be handwaved away when the total state identifies an opportunity to expand its power. With no intermediate spheres of social influence competing for allegiance, the total state can use emergencies to swiftly rationalize exceptions to individual liberty and seize power with little to no resistance.

While it has been all but memory-holed by our media, the Left began the pandemic with a very different attitude towards government action. Early on, Democrats and journalists reacted by characterizing concerns as racist fearmongering over what they saw as a slightly more dangerous than usual flu. California lawmakers encouraged their constituents to attend large celebrations, go out to eat, and, most comically of all, hug an Asian to show they would not fall for xenophobic right-wing propaganda. Speaker of the House Nancy Pelosi even joined local politicians in San Francisco to encourage residents to return to Chinatown and patronize businesses there because local entrepreneurs of Asian descent were going bankrupt due to racist concerns about the virus. The government's point man on the issue, Dr. Anthony Fauci, joined the surgeon general in assuring the public that surgical masks were unnecessary and largely ineffective anyway. Everyone needed to calm down and leave these supplies for the professionals.

As the death toll started to mount and China began extreme mitigation measures like confining the infected to their homes, the narrative shifted. Democrats and most Republicans suddenly supported masking, school closures, lockdowns, and vaccine mandates. Despite initial hesitancy at the federal level, local and state governments led the way in pushing for these precautions, particularly in more progressive states and urban areas. Even as the effectiveness of lockdowns, masking, and vaccinations came into question, the desperation of local and state governments to enforce them only seemed to increase. While some states like Florida eventually adopted an anti-enforcement stance, the media and non-government organizations succeeded in pressuring even staunchly red states to adopt many of the measures.

Internationally, the control that governments could exercise in the name of COVID mitigation appeared almost limitless. Canada made it impossible for the unvaccinated to leave the country. Germany and Austria locked down their unvaccinated, with the latter even making the injection a legal requirement. Australia seemed to return to its roots as a prison colony, beating protesters, arresting families in parks, and placing large numbers of their aboriginal population in detention camps in the name of reducing the spread. Footage of police in Amsterdam turning dogs on "unauthorized" lockdown protesters was shared widely on the internet.

These are, in theory, Western liberal democracies that respect individual rights to assemble, protest, move freely, and have bodily autonomy over medical decisions. Yet those rights quickly vanished as the state moved to consolidate its authority.

The breathtaking expansion of state power continued even as infection and mortality rates plummeted. Goalposts moved at warp speed. Governments that had crafted slogans like "fifteen days to slow the spread" would now inflict years of draconian mitigation efforts. Many stopped even offering end dates for the measures—lockdowns could be of indefinite duration and were marketed as the new normal. Media outlets began churning out think pieces in which journalists, who could barely contain their glee, discussed how lockdowns could be used to address the impact of climate change once the pandemic had passed. Vaccine passports, a measure once mocked by most government and media figures as

hyperbolic far-right scaremongering, were swiftly implemented in many countries and even some American
cities. People were prohibited from flying, using public
transportation, attending public events, going to restaurants, and in some places buying and selling without the
appropriate documentation.

Such punitive measures, had they been implemented
outside of a pandemic and by the leader of a country out
of favor with the liberal international community, such
as Victor Orbán in Hungary, would have generated massive outrage, calls for action from human rights organizations, and economic sanctions. Yet not only did many
Western nations come to exercise tyrannical control over
their citizens, a purity spiral developed as they sought to
implement more extreme lockdowns than their neighbors. An international community that had delivered
countless speeches on the importance of human rights
discarded those rights like used tissue the moment more
power was on the table. The idea that *New York Times*
progressives would admire an Australian policy of placing their native population in detention camps would
have seemed laughable just a few years ago. Now it was
reality.

Again, reductions in infection rates and fatalities
hardly seemed to matter. The argument went from flattening the curve to reducing transmission rates until
vaccines were developed. When the virus continued to
spread despite the vaccines, the standard shifted to the
insane expectation of zero COVID. Compliance with
government mandates and not the actual mitigation of

the sickness became the moral focal point. Experts suggested no masks, then mandatory masking, then double masking, and finally triple masking. Many of the vaccines originally required two shots to be fully effective, then a booster, then two boosters. As experts sprinted from one solution to the next, anyone who expressed even the slightest hesitation over this schizophrenic "medical consensus" was labeled a science-denying conspiracy theorist. Merriam-Webster even took the dystopian step of quietly changing the definition of "anti-vaxxer" in their dictionary from someone who denied the efficacy of vaccines to anyone who opposed the legal enforcement of vaccination requirements.

The fact that a doctrine of individual rights, liberal democracy, and constitutional government in no way inhibited the dynamic expansion of the state would seem to confirm de Jouvenel's assertion about the nature of power. China and America alike demanded incredible levels of control and surveillance, and all of them received it. The only difference was in the narrative required to justify these powers. In the West, the doctrine of individual rights had to be distorted into the "individual right" to not be exposed to a virus or to interact with those who had decided against a particular medical treatment. The fact that these rights had been freshly manufactured and violated the widespread understanding of personal liberties that had existed in the West for centuries seemed to have little effect.

The nature of the situation only became more transparent after the death of George Floyd in police custody in May 2020. The episode sparked nationwide protests, many of which ended in violent riots. Dozens of lives were lost, estimates of property damage reached into the billions, and all of this was allowed, even encouraged, in the middle of a pandemic. Politicians who had spent months talking about the need for people to stay isolated in their homes, who described church services as super-spreader events, were now giving speeches on the importance of turning out in large crowds to express anguish over Floyd's death. While many had been forced to say goodbye to their dying loved ones over the internet, those with the correct political affiliation were allowed to loot and burn cities. The message was clear. Whatever the pretext for lockdowns, vaccine mandates, closures, and the rest, those who were working to support the growing biomedical surveillance state were considered friends, and those who opposed it were enemies. Friends would be granted special privileges, while enemies would be punished at every turn.

The Black Lives Matter riots following Floyd's death were not the only example of criminals being allowed to operate more or less unmolested. Crime spiked all across the country—the violent crime rate, which had been dropping for decades, skyrocketed. Defunding the police became a popular talking point among progressive activists looking to capitalize on the Floyd incident, and those living in areas that took the mantra seriously paid a heavy price.

The theft of items under $9,000 was decriminalized in some parts of California, giving rise to large

shoplifting rings that operated with no fear of consequences. Surveillance videos showed thieves rushing
into stores and clearing shelves as employees looked on
helplessly. The threat of highly transmissible COVID-
19 running through the prison population was used to
justify early release for thousands of prisoners, many of
whom had a history of violent crime and who wasted no
time offending again once they were let out.

Those who had watched their businesses and churches
shut down, their children be confined inside and forced
to learn on a computer, and their holidays get canceled
were shocked. A disturbing conclusion was unavoidable.
The pandemic that they had been made to fear was a
pretense for the expansion of power.

Do not misunderstand: There was a real virus, and it
really was fatal to a small but meaningful percentage of
the population. But that was not how the crisis had been
presented. The public had been threatened with a first
wave that would result in millions of deaths. Experts
painted a picture of crowds dying in the streets because
hospitals would be overflowing with ventilated patients.
Instead, the politically favored were allowed to celebrate
Joe Biden's election victory over Donald Trump while
drinking champagne outside.

This selective application of the law was not
hypocrisy, but the establishment of a new hierarchy.
Conservatives, and those on the right in general, have an
unfortunate habit of pointing out a difference in societal
status, calling it hypocrisy, and thinking that will fix the
problem. This stems from the mistaken belief that the

US Constitution placed all of us on equal footing and effectively limited abuses of government. Conservatives believe pointing out an abuse of power will shame their opponents into returning to the norms of equality. But this is far from the case. Shame requires a shared ethical framework, usually based on religion and modified by social custom. For shame to be effective, the target must have some understanding that what they're doing is wrong and be surrounded by others who apply social pressure until the behavior is corrected.

Progressives do not share the same value system as conservatives beyond some vague overlap in terminology. They believe America is a place of deep inequality, that it has reached its position of privilege due to the immoral exploitation of that inequality, and that any action taken in the pursuit of rectifying that inequality is not just permissible but morally necessary. The system is bigoted in every imaginable way, and so the acquisition of power is always the first priority, as this is the only way to overcome such deeply entrenched injustice.

Progressives think their supporters can and should have rights that exceed those of their opponents. Women, Blacks, Hispanics, and LGTBQ have all been brutally oppressed for centuries. Additional rights are required to combat the hatred and inequality carefully layered into the system by their oppressors. This is nothing new: Those in the civil rights coalition have received an unequal advantage for decades. Affirmative action is a widely accepted legal advantage granted to a minority of the population, even though it violates the stated mutual value of equality. And while a recent Supreme Court ruling did strike down affirmative action preferences that had hindered white and Asian-American admissions at schools like Harvard, it's yet to be seen whether conservatives will be willing to fight to expand this ruling to other institutions like private corporations.

The ability to riot or celebrate in the streets during a pandemic while your political opponents sit locked in their homes is simply an extension of that previously established hierarchy. Those who support the progressive regime are better people. They have historical wrongs to right. They need to go about the work of social justice no matter what the emergency. Their cause is more important than you going to church or sending your children to school.

The doctrine of individual rights has been treated as the moral bedrock of the West since at least 1945, but that has not stopped this rapid expansion of state power. Instead it has often facilitated it. When individual rights enabled government power to liberate the individual from competing social spheres, it was considered convenient, but as soon as it became a hindrance to the further expansion of the state, those rights were redefined without hesitation. The attempt to appeal to a shared principle of individual liberty or equal application of the law by conservatives failed spectacularly because they had assumed they were competing on a level playing field with opponents who had a similar moral framework. It is incredibly important for the American Right to discard that faulty assumption.

There is an even more important failure that must be faced by American conservatives. In the mind of the average Republican voter, the Constitution is a sacred document, carefully designed by the founding fathers to limit the power of the state. It is supposed to serve as a bulwark against the return of the tyrannical government the founders had battled against. Separation of powers, checks and balances, interest set against interest, a deliberate arrangement of opposing forces designed to keep those in charge from obtaining too much power too quickly. But if that is the case, how has government power grown so reliably? How did it explode during the pandemic? If we are to understand the relentless march of the total state, then we will need to explain why the Constitution failed to stop it.

CHAPTER 3

How the Total State Circumvented the Constitution

A merica is very proud of its Constitution. We revere it as a revolutionary document that revived the republican form of government and ushered in a golden age of popular sovereignty. Built on a foundation of progress and enlightenment, it takes a modern and rational understanding of human nature and weaves it into a governmental framework made to stand the test of time. Men would no longer be governed by those who had obtained their positions through accidents of birth. America would have the rule of law, not rule by kings, which would keep power in check. The state would be limited by this carefully designed mechanism, ensuring that individual liberty and sovereignty would be maintained.

As Madison says in the *Federalist Papers*: "Ambition must be made to counteract ambition. The interest of the man must be connected with the constitutional rights of the place. It may be a reflection on human nature, that such devices should be necessary to control the abuses of government. But what is government itself, but the greatest of all reflections of human nature? If men were angels, no government would be necessary. If Angels were to govern men, neither external nor internal controls on government would be necessary. In framing a government which is to be administered by men over men, the great difficulty lies in this: you must first enable government to control the governed; and in the next place oblige it to control itself."[1]

This appeals to our modern sensibilities for a few reasons. First, it feels very clever, like a deep insight into human nature has allowed us to develop a new piece of political technology. It feeds a comforting narrative about progress inevitably leading to an increase in liberty and human flourishing. Second, it puts us in charge of our own destiny. There is nothing above us, no rulers to whom we must pledge our loyalty, no class holding special privilege or responsibility. We are governed by ordinary men just like us, who are constrained by rules just like us, and if we really wanted we could join their ranks at any time. We are not loyal to one man nor governed by one. We are loyal to the system and it's to the system that we turn over power. Because the Constitution is so finely crafted, that system will continue to guard our liberty in perpetuity. There is thus no need to trust a fallible human with our destiny.

Of course, now that we recognize the advance of the total state, we can also recognize an obvious flaw in this

---

1   Madison, *The Federalist Papers*, 51.

narrative. If the Constitution restricts the power of the state, and the power of the state has grown to unprecedented levels, did the Constitution fail or did we fail the Constitution? There are a few ways to answer that question, but let us start by first addressing some of our assumptions about the document's structure.

Political theorist Gaetano Mosca, in his 1939 book *The Ruling Class*, observed that the United States had transformed from a representative republic to an oligarchy operated by a powerful class of bureaucrats. He identified a fundamental misunderstanding of the work of Baron de Montesquieu as a critical reason why the US Constitution had failed to maintain the form of government its creators had intended. Montesquieu was a French philosopher whose work was a major inspiration for the founding fathers. Separation of powers, checks and balances, and most of the other crucial mechanisms woven into Constitution by James Madison and the other framers came from Montesquieu.

Montesquieu was a fan of the English government because it divided power between the king, the parliament, and the courts. He believed that division helped ensure the liberty of the people because each of those sections of government drew power from a different stratum of the nation, and therefore they had competing interests. This tended to naturally limit the power of the state as these interests were always attempting to restrict the power of their rivals. Ambition naturally checked ambition, as Madison would later echo in the *Federalist Papers*, and this meant the interests of one group were rarely allowed to dominate at the expense of the others for long.

Americans took this model and applied it to our own three branches of government, giving each separate powers and the ability to limit the actions of the other two. The problem Mosca identified with the modern American interpretation of Montesquieu was that it focused far too much on the mechanical aspects of the system and not on why it actually worked. People are not machines even if your average political scientist or bureaucrat would like to treat them that way, and neither are the governments they create. Those who treat governments like machines make fundamental errors as to how and why political events take place.

The magic of mixed government is not contained in the fact that three is some kind of special number that creates a stable pyramid of state. Three, five, seven branches—the number is not as important as what they represent. In the last chapter, we learned from de Jouvenel that competing spheres of social influence are what hold the natural expansion of government at bay. Thus, the only thing that can moderate this expansion is other social forces that command the loyalty of the citizenry. The branches were meant to represent these different social forces, thereby forcing different constituencies to come to the table and negotiate.

Why don't America's three branches represent different social spheres that draw their power from a diverse set of organizing interests? Mosca blames mass democracy. America originally only allowed one half of one third of the federal government to be elected directly by the people. This meant that aristocratic and regional powers had far more control over the ruling apparatus. Even those parts of government that were directly subject to the democratic process were selected by a very narrow group of voting citizens. With the direct election of senators, the creation of presidential primaries, and the vast expansion of the franchise, the nature of how the government was selected was fundamentally altered.

With the introduction of mass democracy, every branch was now subject to the same selective force: public opinion. Control of information and manipulation of public perception were now the only necessary levers of power. Those best able to control the opinions and passions of the electorate would dominate all three branches of American government. Even the judiciary, which in theory is the branch most insulated from the whims of the electorate, is selected by the president and approved by the legislature, both of which are now completely dependent on public sentiment. Oligarchs, with their financial ability to influence mass media, education, and marketing, quickly proved to be the social force most able to manipulate the public will. With all three branches now functionally subject to the same democratic selection pressures, it is no surprise an oligarchy came to achieve hegemonic social force in the United States.

Mosca writes:

They have often forgotten that if one political institution is to be an effective curb upon the activity of another it must represent a political force—it must, that is, be the organized expression of a social influence and a social authority that has some standing in the community, as against the forces that are expressed in the political institution that is to be controlled. That is why, in certain parliamentary monarchies, in spite of the letter of the constitutions and fundamental charters, we see head of states, who are supported neither by ancient traditions nor by the all but vanishing precedent of the divine-right doctrine nor by the influence of the bureaucracy, the army of the economically superior classes, becoming powerless to counterbalance the influence of elective assemblies, who are supported by a belief that they represent the totality of the citizens and actually comprise within themselves a considerable body of capacities, interests, ambitions, and energies. That is why in those same countries the courts are proclaimed by word of mouth to be fundamental organs of the state, while in fact they are mere branches of a bureaucracy, depending upon a cabinet that is loyal to the majority in the elective chamber. So they come to lack prestige and independence and are never capable of mustering enough moral and intellectual energy to assert their own importance.[2]

---

2   Mosca, *The Ruling Class*, p. 138.

Despite Mosca focusing on a parliamentary democracy in this passage, we can see the parallels to our own system. The executive and judicial branches become bureaucracies in service to the legislative branch. When popular sovereignty is the only legitimating force in society, the most democratically elected branch is seen as the most valid. It makes all other branches subservient and they are eventually made subject to the exact same selection pressures. No other social force is considered legitimate, and so manipulation of public opinion becomes the key to ruling the entire state.

As we pointed out in the first chapter, maintaining power in a democratic system means maintaining control over how the populace perceives and understands the world around them. As each branch of government becomes more vulnerable to the democratic process, control of power hinges increasingly on the ability to manipulate the masses. Instead of different societal forces with different bases of power being forced to the table and checking each other's interests, power becomes dependent on one source: public opinion. The ability to wield power is reduced to an arms race around perfecting one skill: the manipulation of public opinion. The ability to direct massive quantities of capital allows oligarchs to simultaneously own entertainment companies and news outlets while funding educational institutions and political campaigns. With the collapse of religious, aristocratic, and tribal power, monied and managerial interests are the only ones allowed to elevate elites within the hierarchy. Oligarchy becomes the only force capable of simultaneously influencing mass media, mass education, and mass bureaucracy, which are the key levers of power for influencing mass democracy. All three branches quickly fall under the influence of oligarchical domination.

We now understand why the separation of powers failed to keep the interests of the different government branches from unifying, but that's not the only defense against tyranny that the Constitution erects. Limits on government power are intentionally written into the articles of the Constitution and the Bill of Rights, so we also need to explain why those explicit protections failed in the face of the total state. For that, we will need to turn to a different political theorist: Joseph de Maistre.

No one likes the notion of being ruled, especially Americans. We want to be masters of our own fate, free to pursue happiness and prosperity as we see fit. Despite this impulse, we also know some level of organized state is required, so we put our faith in the rule of law, a clearly outlined set of rules that everyone, even our leaders, must follow. This emphasis on a rule-based order is supposed to protect us from the caprice of individual leaders and constrain their tendency to abuse power. De Maistre, however, reminds us there is no escaping rule by individuals, no matter how clever we think we are in constructing a constitution.

Modern Western people tend to see laws in a very simplistic way. There are rules, you write down those rules, and once they are written down everyone must follow those rules. If you violate those rules, you will be held accountable because they are written down for everyone to see. But de Maistre explains that laws have a far more complex and organic origin and that formally inscribing them into a constitution can actually have significant drawbacks:

> The more you examine the part human action plays in the formation of political constitutions, the clearer it becomes that it is effective only in an extremely subordinate role or as a simple instrument; and I do not believe that any doubt at all remains of the incontrovertible truth of the following propositions:
>
> 1. That the fundamentals of political constitutions exist before all written laws.
> 2. That a constitutional law is and can be only the development or the sanction of a preexistent and unwritten right.
> 3. That the most essential, the most intrinsically constitutional, and the really fundamental is not written and even should not be if the state is not to be imperiled.
> 4. That the weakness and fragility of a constitution is in direct relationship to the number of written constitutional articles.[3]

De Maistre believes that constitutions do not by themselves create the cultural norms, laws, and institutions

---

3   De Maistre, *Major Works* "Essay on the Generative Principle of Political Constitutions," IX.

that rule over a people. Instead, they simply formal-ize those that have already arisen naturally out of the character of the people. The true meaning of laws and constitutions cannot be captured on paper because the true meaning exists in the context of the people and the society that created them. They can only be truly under-stood in the lived experience of the culture from which they were naturally derived. It is the common nature of the people, the shared frame of reference, that creates the actual meaning of laws and constitutions.

"The more that is written, the weaker is the institu-tion, the reason being clear," writes de Maistre. "Laws are only declarations of rights, and rights are not declared except when they are attacked, so that the multiplicity of the written constitutional laws shows only the multiplic-ity of conflicts and the danger of destruction . . . No nation can give itself liberty if it has not it already. Its laws are made when it begins to reflect on itself."[4]

That the effectiveness of the constitution is closely bound to the character and culture of the people for whom it is written was something the founding fathers understood better than modern Americans. John Adams famously stated that the Constitution was meant for a moral and religious people and would be inadequate to govern a nation of a different character. The Declaration of Independence states that "We find these truths to be self-evident." But how can any moral truth be self-evident

---

4   De Maistre, *Major Works*, "Considerations On France," Ch 6.8.

unless the people who are observing it share the same value system?

Many ancient civilizations, including some we think of as very advanced like the Romans, regularly left unwanted infants to die of exposure. This was not seen as particularly immoral or barbaric. Two people from different cultures looking at an apple falling from a tree might agree that it is self-evident that dropped objects fall to the surface of the earth. But they might then look at a baby being left to perish and see very different things, and both will assume what they see as self-evident. This is not to argue for moral relativism, but to recognize that different populations with different cultures will make different moral assumptions, be they right or wrong, and that the governments of those nations must take their character into account in order to rule successfully.

Without a similar basis for both logic and morality, no shared culture can be formed. This is why de Maistre says what makes a nation or a people cannot be captured on paper. Written laws may be a necessary evil, but we should not assume that simply because something is on paper it becomes inviolable. It can be quite the opposite. Relying too heavily on a written constitution simply incentivizes a nation's leaders to become skilled at twisting and shaping language in order to circumvent the restrictions created by the formal meaning of its words.

"Man cannot make a constitution, and no legitimate constitution can be written," says de Maistre. "The corpus of fundamental laws that must constitute a civil or religious society have never been and never will be written. This can be done only when the society is already constituted, yet it is impossible to spell out or explain in writing certain individual articles; but almost always these declarations are the effect or the cause of very great evils and they always cost the people more than they are worth."[5]

Many today would mock de Maistre's assertion that constitutions are divinely inspired and are carried out in a religious fashion. The idea that only religion can bind a people into a constitutional order would probably get you laughed out of the average political science department. But those same professors would then go about their day living according to a cultural constitution that very clearly reflects a progressive worldview. Establishing the binding faith of your society in materialism does not mean you have escaped the human need to ground your constitution in religion. You have simply redefined your terms.

The modern obsession with progress, rationality, systems, and proceduralism has made us forget what a constitution is. Constitutions are a reflection of the spirit, nature, and culture of the people who live under them. A constitution is not some ironclad contract that cures the human condition. It is not a piece of political technology that solves the problem of a fallen humanity. When Americans started treating the Constitution as

---

5   De Maistre, *Major Works*, "Essay on the Generative Principles of Political Constitutions," XVIII.

the soul of our nation, they naturally fell into a hollow proceduralism.

With the metaphysical underpinnings of the nation now dependent on a dry and dusty document instead of a living and vibrant tradition, a new animating spirit rushed in and filled the void. This was the progressive spirit many call "wokeness." It's what happens when you pretend the responsibility to pass down a people's values and culture can be delegated to a system. The animating spirit of the nation must be actively renewed by each generation. If those who interpret and apply the Constitution do not believe in and live out the values it embodies, the paper itself has no hope of stopping the total state.

We now better understand the limits of a constitution and why America's founding documents could never prevent the total state on their own. But to better grasp how the United States slowly transformed from a limited constitutional republic to a total state, we are going to need to look at a controversial political theorist who expanded on the work of Joseph de Maistre.

CHAPTER 4

How Liberalism Obfuscated the Growth of the Total State

T he state will plan a perfect economy in which every citizen works the fewest hours necessary and everyone receives what they need. The people, freed from their slavery to exploitative labor, will have time to write epic poetry and paint magnificent works of art. This will lead to a grand explosion of culture and usher in an earthly utopia.

This fantasy of communism is something most Americans would readily dismiss. It's a founding myth that makes ridiculous assumptions that could never come to fruition in the real world. At its core, communism relies on a faulty understanding of human nature that dooms it from the outset. But most Americans don't ever stop to question whether liberal democracy makes similarly outlandish assumptions.

In order to identify the flaws in our own founding myth, we turn now to the work of Carl Schmitt. And in order to delve into Carl Schmitt, we need to first understand two things. First, when we refer to liberalism in this chapter, we do not mean it in the contemporary American political context of progressive Democrats and their political priorities. We are referring to what is commonly called classical liberalism, including the idea that the political leadership of a country is selected by a democratic process of debates and elections. Second, we need to address the fact that Schmitt was a member of the National Socialist Party of Germany (so was Wernher von Braun but his ideas got America to the moon). This is deeply unfortunate, but if we want to better understand the flaws of our own system it helps to see it from the outside, and Schmitt, whatever his very serious faults, is one of the most effective critics of the liberal understanding of politics. So we'll take what is valuable and leave the rest.

In his book *The Concept of the Political*, Schmitt asserts that the idea of a large group of people with mutually exclusive values and radically different cultures coming together and working out all of their differences through an exchange of ideas is, on its face, an unrealistic fantasy. Any belief that would threaten the existence of a group is by definition non-negotiable for that group. Having been raised in liberal democracies, we have been trained to see many defining features of our groups as negotiable, or have been taught that we do not exist in a particular group at all. But for Schmitt, these non-negotiable features are common and existential conflicts happen all the time whether we recognize them as such or not.

According to Schmitt, politics is not some separate realm where debates about policy take place. It is a state that any disagreement about group identity can reach, be it economic, religious, or tribal. This is where Schmitt's infamous friend/enemy distinction is born. As soon as any key aspect of a group's identity comes under dispute, that group by necessity creates a distinction that divides friend from enemy. The marker may be a spiritual belief, economic status, or political policy, but those on one side of the line become friends and those on the other side are enemies. Schmitt sees the friend/enemy distinction as the fundamental organizing principle of politics and says all other distinctions that exist while forming political coalitions are subordinate.

Differences in opinion or priority may exist inside the friend coalition, but everyone who has been identified as a friend does not threaten the core story that is vital to the identity of the group. By the same token, the political enemy may not be morally evil. In the past, it may have even been advantageous to do business with him. But having now been defined as a threat to the friendly coalition, the enemy is alien and hostile in a way that could justify conflict. The enemy is not simply a competitor, but left unchecked could destroy those identified as friends.

Liberalism promised to remove the friend/enemy distinction, essentially removing politics from the political. It attempted to achieve this by putting on a show of civil debates, introducing a marketplace of ideas where people in nice suits would deliver speeches on how differences would be overcome and consensus would be reached. The rapidly increasing viciousness of our own political discourse helps us see through this illusion better than previous generations were able to. Americans in the past may have had a hard time recognizing the friend/enemy distinction operating in the background as well-mannered orators exchanged carefully rehearsed replies on network television, but modern politicians lack the self-control to hide that conflict. Today, politicians and pundits routinely declare their opponents to be traitors, terrorists, and insurrectionists. Suggesting they should be imprisoned is commonplace.

Even when those in power were more disciplined, this was always an illusion. Schmitt says such carefully choreographed negotiations have always been window-dressing meant to obfuscate the continuing battle for control between friend and enemy that rages behind the scenes. Despite the comforting fiction of the marketplace of ideas where only the best policies were supposed to emerge victorious, it is increasingly clear that policies advantageous to the ruling groups and their interests win no matter what.

Schmitt argues that liberalism attempts to reduce or remove aspects of group identities in an attempt to reduce areas of competition for the friend/enemy distinction. Liberalism pushes relentlessly toward globalization and homogenization across boundaries in its attempt to control an increasing number of people without having to navigate or resolve political conflict. This may remind you of the total state removing the competing social spheres that hinder its expansion. That is because they are one and the same.

Liberalism, with its promise to eliminate existential political conflict and replace it with objectively beneficial governance, serves as the perfect narrative justification for the expansion of the total state. But the total state does not eliminate the friend/enemy distinction because that is impossible. Instead, it seeks to become the only entity with the authority to define the terms of the friend/enemy distinction for an ever-expanding ideological empire. Those who serve to strengthen the power of the state are friends, while those who seek to compete with or restrain it are the enemy.

This critical insight on the nature of liberalism shatters another conceit on which the total state relies: the myth of the neutral institution. Liberalism advanced the notion that the conflict of moral vision that drives the friend/enemy distinction could be removed by appealing to a value-free and objective set of rational actors. Any notion of the metaphysical would be rejected in favor of a focus on efficiency and tasks that could be quantified scientifically and judged by objective criteria. A school could teach children to read and solve math equations, measure their aptitude for those tasks by assessing data, and credential them without needing to adhere to any specific moral code or religious doctrine. A corporation could produce goods, market them, and sell them to anyone, reaping a profit for their investors regardless of their race or creed. A government could deliver services and administer justice without addressing the larger questions that in the past had driven humanity to conflict.

Modern neutral institutions are an incredibly useful fiction for the total state because they set the populace at ease, reducing the scrutiny applied to power. People like the idea that they rule themselves, but they hate putting in the work. Constantly monitoring and pushing back against powerful institutions is difficult, dangerous, and, most importantly, tedious. If the state is addressing existential questions that could threaten a community and its way of life, then being aware of who rules you and what they value is critical. But if powerful institutions are politically neutral, there is no need to monitor them. And if those institutions have had their interests set against each other, providing checks and balances, so much the better.

Schmitt helps us to understand that this kind of neutrality is impossible. Institutions are run by men, not pieces of paper, and men always have interests, groups, and moral visions to which they are loyal. The effects may be subtle at first, but those in power will always identify friends and enemies, will always introduce the political, and will always reward and punish. No act of production, oversight, or administration is value-free. A moral vision will inform the procedures and goals of every institution. It is not a question of whether someone's priorities will guide the function of the organization; it is only a question of whose priorities will reign supreme. The total state relies on the myth of the neutral institution to obfuscate the advance of its own values inside the key structures of civilization.

Like de Jouvenel, Schmitt recognizes popular sovereignty as a key factor in the rise of the total state. When the state had a monopoly on politics, its corrosive influence was confined to that domain. Different social spheres like church, community, and family could remain apolitical because control of them was unnecessary for the state to maintain power. These institutions could assert influence and demand loyalty inside their own spheres. With the rise of democracy as the legitimating mechanism of state, total control of all social institutions became essential to the centralization of power.

As Schmitt says, "The equation state = politics becomes erroneous and deceptive at exactly the moment when state and society penetrate each other. What had been up to that point affairs of state become thereby social matters, and vice versa, what had been purely social matters become affairs of state—as must necessarily occur in a democratically organized unit. Heretofore ostensibly neutral domains—religion, culture, education, the economy—then cease to be neutral in the sense that they do not pertain to state and to politics. As a polemical concept against such neutralizations and depoliticizations of important domains appears the total state, which potentially embraces every domain. This results in the identity of state and society. In such a state, therefore, everything is at least potentially political, and in referring to the state it is no longer possible to assert for it a specifically political characteristic."[1]

Schmitt also makes a valuable contribution to our political understanding with a powerful tool for

---

1   Schmitt, *The Concept of the Political*, p. 22.

recognizing sovereignty. Sovereignty is a funny word for those living in the modern West. It's often used, particularly in old stories about ancient kings, but we rarely think about how it applies today. In a modern democracy, we are not ruled by powerful kings or sovereigns. Contemporary nations have popular sovereignty. The people rule, and so there is less need to think about who wields supreme authority. Which is very convenient for those who actually do wield supreme authority.

In his book *Political Theology*, Schmitt outlines a clear and direct method for identifying who holds political sovereignty in a nation. "The sovereign is he who decides on the exception."[2] As we have established previously, there is no perfectly designed system of government that anticipates and protects against all contingencies. There is no constitution, no outline for government power, that can include the exception. All civilizations will encounter unforeseeable circumstances where exceptions to the prescribed order must be made. And the system by definition cannot predict all these exceptions. No matter how carefully crafted its structure, no matter how many contingencies it attempts to anticipate, it can never encompass every possible crisis and its required response. Unexpected emergencies will arise, and far more often than we moderns are willing to admit.

When they do, we tend to rationalize away the exceptions that are necessarily made. In exploring this,

2   Schmitt, *Political Theology*, p.5.

Schmitt draws on the works of thinkers like Joseph de Maistre who focus on the decision-making function of sovereignty. As citizens of liberal democracies, we have been trained to be wary of decisive leadership in our government, even though we value it in basically every other walk of life. Deliberation makes us feel more comfortable in times of stability, but when things hit the fan, everyone instinctually craves decisive leadership.

Such decisive leadership is a very rare and valuable characteristic. In the modern world, we are taught that the design of our government allows us to escape the need for it, and we like that because it frees us from the dependence implied by its necessity. If the system is in charge, then sovereignty is distributed and the individual is freed from obligations to a single ruler. But this is a comforting fiction. We never escape the need for decisive leadership—someone is always in charge. Even if we are told we are ruled by a system, those who decide on the exceptions to that system are the ones who hold sovereignty.

Liberalism once again attempts to obfuscate this by replacing sovereignty with procedure. But proceduralism cannot anticipate the exceptions to the liberal process. At best a constitution can designate who is responsible for acting when the exception arises.

Today we associate the word dictator with an evil tyrant, but in ancient Rome the dictator was an official legal office. In times of emergency, normal republican government was suspended and total sovereignty was invested in one leader for a limited period of time. The dictator was given total authority to solve the crisis that had made his appointment necessary, with normal government resuming once the emergency had ended and the exception was no longer necessary. But, of course, nothing except honor, and the possibility of assassination, compelled the dictator to cede his power.

Schmitt sees the state as a secularization of theology. By acting as the sovereign, determining hierarchies, and handing down law, the state mirrors the role of metaphysical deity, translating its relationship with the people into temporal institutions. This is where the exception finds its origin, and Schmitt ties the state of exception to the theological idea of the miracle. The sovereign who created the laws of the universe decides when those laws can be suspended and an exception, or miracle, can take place. The same can be said for a government whose day-to-day processes may be set in place, but that can always be interrupted by those who actually hold power in the name of an exception.

Schmitt also links the attempt to limit sovereignty through constitutional protections to the attempt to remove miracles from theology. He argues that the modern liberal constitutional state springs from deism. In many ways, deism was a theological attempt to remove miracles as a necessary component from explanations of how the universe functioned. Deism also just so happened to be a very popular intellectual movement when America's founders were writing its Constitution. The rationalism of the Enlightenment compelled many thinkers to create totalizing systems that removed the need for exceptions from both religion and politics.

Schmitt writes, "Although the liberal bourgeoisie wanted a god, its god could not become active; it wanted a monarch, but he had to be powerless; it demanded freedom and equality but limited voting rights to the propertied classes in order to ensure the influence of education and property on legislation, as if education and property entitled that class to repress the poor and uneducated; it abolished the aristocracy of blood and family but permitted the impudent rule of the moneyed aristocracy, the most ignorant and the most ordinary form of an aristocracy; it wanted neither the sovereignty of the king nor that of the people."[3]

Despite all of their attempts to perfect their governing system, liberals were unable to remove the need for sovereignty from politics. The necessity of deciding on the exception continued to persist. No system can remove the need for a sovereign, but it can make the function more confusing and ineffective. Systems always break down, they always have limits, and when those limits are reached someone must always wield power.

What complicated systems *can* do is obfuscate the process, reducing the accountability of individual actors, and this is the utility of liberalism to the ruling class. Liberal democracy does an amazing job of dissipating accountability, spreading it across the entire system, which is difficult to hold accountable. By placing the

---

3   Schmitt, *Political Theology*, p.60.

powerful behind the faceless shroud of democracy, the ruling class can shield itself from the consequences of their own actions. Exceptions can be made that benefit the rulers at the cost of the ruled, and in a democracy the people have only each other to blame because those who truly wield power are tucked safely out of view.

As we have seen, there is no one person in charge of the total state. There is not even one shadowy cabal with an official roster of members. The Cathedral is an entire class and it will be the central topic of the next few chapters.

CHAPTER 5

Foxes, Lions, and the Total State

When people imagine a total state, they usually envision a dystopian science fiction novel full of jackbooted thugs and gulags. This is understandable, as the total states of the early twentieth century like Nazi Germany and the Soviet Union prominently featured brutal violence and mass imprisonment as their main enforcement mechanisms.

The close association of totalitarianism with violence in the popular consciousness can, however, mislead us into believing that a system without direct and omnipresent violent oppression is free. Many will point to the lack of prison camps or storm troopers as evidence that America isn't really approaching a total state. But Aldous Huxley's novel *Brave New World* should remind us there is an entirely different form of power that can be used to control a society. In contrast to the brute force in George Orwell's *Nineteen Eighty-Four*, Huxley's dystopia relies more on scientific manipulation, indoctrination, and bureaucracy to control the population while being no less totalitarian.

In this chapter, we will examine the two main types of ruling elite, the different forms of power they wield, and how their character impacts the ways in which they control the population.

In his book *The Prince*, Niccolo Machiavelli suggests that rulers emulate two types of animals: foxes and lions. Lions are strong and courageous, capable of fighting off wolves and protecting their pride, but they can easily be caught in a trap. Foxes are clever and cunning, able to maneuver out of difficult situations and avoid traps, but they have no hope in a direct fight with a pack of wolves.

The political theorist and sociologist Vilfredo Pareto would later expand on these categories, describing the characteristics, attitudes, and motivations of what he called class one residues (foxes) and class two residues (lions). Pareto's nomenclature is particular to his much larger system of sociology, which is fascinating but not germane to our topic. While we will be drawing heavily from Pareto's work, we will keep Machiavelli's classifications of foxes and lions for the sake of simplicity.

Lions are strong, patriotic, and courageous. They value order and are naturally conservative, with a strong interest in preserving the traditions and forms of their society. Ruling elites with a lion disposition generally invest in institutions that generate stability, perpetuate hierarchy, and communicate shared values to subsequent generations. They encourage the persistence of kin groups, recognize the existence and duties of different social classes, and value loyalty very highly. These leaders also tend towards the continuation of ideas that define their societies, including those that are formally religious like gods and organized churches, as well as those that are informally religious such as the celebration of heroes and the noble dead who defended the nation. Lions are generally found in the martial class. They are natural leaders who rise to challenges through acts of bravery and skill in combat.

Foxes are clever, crafty, and nimble. They are very skilled at the manipulation of ideas. Ruling elites of the fox disposition are always seeking new knowledge, new ways to approach a situation, and new tools to address the issues their societies might face. They encourage their people to take risks, embrace new technologies, build new institutions, and expand their horizons. Foxes are not necessarily attached to what currently is. They are happy to combine, rearrange, or completely replace institutions without worrying much about the consequences. These are the leaders who transform economic systems and transition civilizations from one form of production to another. Foxes tend to be intellectuals, businessmen, media figures, and those who otherwise benefit from the manipulation of ideas and data.

When a civilization is in its infancy, lions dominate. A new tribe or nation must fight for its existence, defining itself and securing control of its borders. New civilizations are constantly addressing the kinds of challenges for which lions are best suited. Lions ably provide physical security and are highly capable when it comes to bringing order inside the borders of the state. If crime has risen to unacceptable levels or political unrest has turned violent, the people look to lions to correct the problem. The ruling class is usually dominated by lions if the nation is often at war. The leadership of lions is also very valuable in expansionist phases when exploration, colonization, and wars of acquisition are required.

As societies become more complex and the problems they face become more abstract, foxes tend to dominate. Once physical safety has become less of a day-to-day struggle and security can be expected in most circumstances, the structure of a civilization becomes more sophisticated. Specialization and expertise emerge, which only compound the growth of complex and interdependent networks. The need for overwhelming physical force wanes, and the demand for the manipulation and combination of sophisticated ideas rises significantly. Large-scale coordination requires new forms of organization, mass communication, and economy, areas in which foxes excel.

It is important to acknowledge that no ruling class is composed of all foxes or all lions. Pareto notes it is important to have a mix of both types in your ruling elite at all stages, and Machiavelli suggests it is important for individual leaders to have a healthy mix of both of these spirits. When we discuss the tendencies of various groups, we should remember they are still made up of individuals who are making decisions. We can see shared interests and trends that unlock insights about the nature of a ruling elite, but individuals can still act outside of or completely disrupt these stereotypes. Julius Caesar was a brilliant military leader who also possessed a unique gift for politics and manipulation. The great men of history have often radically remade the paradigms of power in their own image, at least for a time.

When a society is ruled through physical violence, you can be sure that lions will dominate. With our very modern aversion to overt force, we might see this as the worst option, but that is not necessarily the case. Whether we are comfortable admitting it or not, all societies are implicitly governed by the threat of force. Peaceful navigation of the social hierarchy can only occur once violence has been removed as an option, and violence is only removed as an option when one individual or class of individuals has gained a monopoly over it. As Robert Heinlein famously put it in his novel *Starship Troopers*, "Force, my friends, is violence. The supreme authority from which all other authorities are derived." Those who forget this basic truth always pay dearly. Until peace has been secured through a monopoly on violence, no higher functions of society can be addressed and no more abstract goods acquired. Societies dominated by crafty foxes still rest on the monopoly on force, even if that power is obfuscated by many layers of abstraction and rarely used.

While no one enjoys being ruled by the regular application of direct force, this is not usually necessary. Lions tend to ensure that when such force is utilized, it's swift, targeted, and effective. This is why lions are generally valued in areas like law and order where the consistent and efficient application of force yields more reliable results than clever manipulation. The talent of lions for keeping a strict hold on order is also more valuable when a civilization is facing existential threats from outside its borders. Nations that are engaged in a life-or-death struggle with foreign powers do not have the luxury of being tolerant of rampant criminal behavior at home. They tend to value the reliable production of a large and competent martial caste, which tends to accompany rule by lions.

While rule by lions has obvious advantages, it also tends to have hard limits. As the problems that civilizations face become more complex and abstract, the effective application of force, as valuable as it might be, becomes a less reliable solution. As the nation becomes more powerful and subdues its nearby enemies, it is no longer in immediate need of a large and highly competent martial caste. Its problems tend to become issues of scale and exchange, more likely to be solved by the clever manipulation of existing systems or the creation of entirely new ones. When security ceases to be the central concern of a civilization, increasing coordination and facilitating the generation of surplus starts to take precedence. The fox's natural inclination to seek out new approaches, alongside his skill at creating new concepts through manipulation, gradually leads him to dominate the ruling class of societies undergoing this shift.

While foxes still rely on the implicit threat of force, they are neither skilled at nor comfortable with its regular application. This does not mean, however, that foxes do not bend their populations to their will. All ruling classes need a way to guide the behavior of the masses—this is what makes them the rulers. The lack of competent displays of force by the foxes does not mean the people are free of elite influence; it simply means that different forms of influence are being utilized.

Foxes tend to rule through deceit. Just as no ruling class maintains control without a monopoly on force, no ruling class stays in power without an ideological justification for their position. Due to their lack of raw displays of force, foxes tend to lean heavily on the manipulation of systems along with the subtle control of information and data to maintain order. Advanced civilizations require foxes to operate the complex systems on which they are dependent, and this expertise factors heavily into the political formula of the foxes. While it may not be as brutal and jarring as open displays of violence, it is just as capable of becoming totalitarian.

Most of the totalitarian regimes of the last century have understood the importance of controlling information and shaping the narrative that legitimates their power. In Nazi Germany and Soviet Russia, this control was achieved through obvious propaganda, but was also delivered through the brutal application of force, which is what we generally default to when we think of a total state. Western liberal democracies may have forgone the regular displays of violence, but they also understand the essential nature of narrative control, especially in the age of mass media and mass production. As we noted in chapter one, journalist Walter Lippman made the case that the public must be manipulated by the media and other elite opinion makers so they do not vote foolishly, and that lesson was taken to heart. Mass media is a powerful tool for shaping the beliefs of the nation, and good liberals like Lippman understood it as their duty to guide popular sovereignty to the correct conclusions using the power of the press.

The Cathedral, which serves as the decentralized consensus-manufacturing apparatus for the United States and the wider Western world, has proven a far more effective and durable version of mass narrative control. While the Nazis and Soviets achieved ideological hegemony in a far more immediate fashion, their rule also proved brittle. The tight grip of the lions in those societies drove them to collapse, but in the liberal West, the gradual approach of the foxes proved more resilient.

Despite the lack of gulags or internment camps, people in liberal democracies are increasingly terrified to speak their minds. In Orwell's *Nineteen Eighty-Four*, the public enemy is subjected to Two Minutes Hate, but in modern Western regimes the human sacrifice can go on much longer. An errant word on social media or an awkward interaction at work can end a person's career and make them the target of a public hate campaign that will strip away their friends and family. The progressive outrage machine combs through every human interaction seeking out wrongthink. The impressive part is that the machine trains the population to do most of the monitoring and policing for it.

Punishing dissent in traditionally totalitarian societies may be effective, but it also tends to be messy and draws attention directly to its source. If a regime plans to cart off dissidents to an internment camp and execute them, that will probably deter any further dissent, but the downsides are obvious. The constant need to apply brutal violence is jarring and tends to wear on the populace, the logistics are a nightmare, and, worst of all for those in power, the chain of accountability is clear. The guys showing up with guns are clearly working on behalf of the state. The officer ordering their actions is clearly responsible for what took place. If the people ever decide to rise up and hold someone accountable, they know exactly who to blame.

The fox's approach to totalitarian social control is much slower and requires far more patience, but it has many advantages. While the Cathedral is constantly advancing progressive ideology through educational, cultural, and corporate institutions, its decentralized nature makes it far more difficult to pinpoint the source of the totalitarian dogma. The ideological dictates feel more organic because they accumulate slowly and appear to emerge from the normal processes of the institutions around the citizen rather than being directly issued from an official organ of the state. By making a nameless, faceless, ever-shifting process the agent of totalitarian oppression, rulers can obfuscate the source of power and how it is actually applied. It is almost impossible to hold a process accountable, especially when the mechanisms of that process are easily manipulated by an unspecified ruling elite.

Democracy is also a useful tool for an elite interested in implementing soft totalitarianism without being held accountable. The idea of popular sovereignty conditions people to believe the masses select their leaders and hold them accountable. This means that while an individual might be able to identify a leader they disagree with, that leader is only one of many and never solely responsible. And even if that leader could be singled out as the cause of totalitarian action, it is ultimately the duty of the citizens to hold him accountable. When elections fail to do this, it effectively shifts the blame to the voters themselves. The ruling elite are, in theory, simply the servants of the people, and if only those red/blue state voters were not so evil/stupid, then the system would work correctly.

The abuse of the public/private distinction has also been key to the implementation of soft totalitarianism by the foxes, particularly in the United States. American citizens are taught at a very young age that the government is constrained by the mechanisms of the Constitution and the Bill of Rights, but these restrictions do not apply to private organizations. This emphasis is understandable given the country's origins, but the idea that the powers of the state and of private entities are completely separable is a mistake. As we discussed earlier, the Cathedral derives its authority from its ability to coordinate across multiple organizations, both public and private. The Pentagon, the *New York Times*, Harvard, Facebook, and Apple all think in lockstep and are all eager to wield their influence despite only one of them being a formal government institution.

All these institutions will fire someone for disagreeing with them publicly. Most of them will actively seek the destruction of those outside their immediate employ for dissent. This is commonly called "cancel culture" by its opponents, but such terrible branding hides the true exercise of power. By characterizing the public destruction of a wrongthinking individual as culture, foxes are able to once again disperse the responsibility. There is no one individual to be held accountable; it is the culture at large that is to blame. No one can hold a culture accountable and changing an entire culture is a monumental task, so once again the cost of exercising power for the foxes ends up dissipated.

The larger and more complex this network of social and economic infrastructure becomes, and the more reliant civilization is upon it, the more avenues the foxes have to exercise totalitarianism without accountability. Once again, the COVID pandemic provides exceptional examples of how soft power, with the aid of key technological advancements, provides a reach that most dictators could only dream of. Before looking at how fox-style elites used COVID to exercise an insane level of power, one must understand the kind of technological and supply networks required for this to even become an option.

First, there needs to be a media apparatus so powerful and so omnipresent that it can make a nasty flu look like the Black Death. Social media and twenty-four-hour news coverage must thrust a narrative of apocalyptic proportions in front of people who are mostly experiencing mild cold symptoms and force them to believe it. Total social isolation helps, but this is still an impressively

complex undertaking that requires sophisticated propaganda delivery techniques. Elites also need a supply
chain capable of facilitating at-home work, education,
entertainment, and food delivery if they want to maintain the illusion. Anyone who must regularly leave home
to go to work, school, or the grocery store will be less
likely to buy the delusion. Without a populace already
conditioned to consume a large amount of electronic
entertainment, individuals will become restless and defy
government dictates.

Make no mistake: not everyone can sit at home. Much
of the working class is still required to go outside and
keep the wheels of civilizations turning. The point is not
to lock down everyone but to lock down the right people.
An infrastructure built on Netflix, Amazon, DoorDash,
and automated grocery curbside pickup allowed mid-
dle- and upper-class information-based workers to stay
locked down without disturbing the most essential parts
of their lifestyle. These are the people with the most
social influence and the ones most capable of pushing
back, so controlling them properly is essential.

Technology not only allows these essential classes to
remain propagandized and locked down for an extended
period of time, it facilitates the large-scale management
of dissent. Social media can identify medical experts willing to speak out against the narrative, censor them, and
mark them for exile by the relevant professional organizations. The threat of constant video surveillance via the
camera present in the pocket of almost every human in
the developed world assures large-scale compliance with

requirements like mask mandates. A skeptic might find the need to wear a mask outside ridiculous, but footage of him having an argument with an aggressive pro-mask stranger could ensure he's fired from his job the next day. In Australia, regional governments created smartphone apps requiring anyone under quarantine to regularly take pictures of themselves and confirm their location to prove compliance. When truck drivers in Canada protested vaccine mandates by peacefully shutting down their nation's capital and a few border crossings, the government seized money that had been donated to fund their demonstration and froze the bank accounts of those who had contributed.

In the end, even with technological advancements and financial manipulation, the application of force was sometimes necessary. The few Canadian truckers who continued to protest were hauled off of a bridge in handcuffs after a healthy dose of state-administered violence. Footage of Australian police trampling protesters with horses and arresting families who dared to visit empty beaches or parks went viral. Despite unrest raging for months during the pandemic, Washington, D.C. was put under what amounted to a military occupation only after a protest at the Capitol building on January 6, 2021 ended with participants entering and taking pictures. As much as foxes can rely on propaganda and procedural manipulation, they will use force when soft power reaches its natural limits.

This application of force is usually treated as a last resort for a few reasons. Soft power is hard to see and

harder to locate. The foxes that dominate the West rely
on the notion that their dictates are rational, organic,
and largely voluntary to provide an illusion of liberty.
No one is being forced at gunpoint to comply with arbi-
trary government orders; they are being encouraged to
follow the science through cultural and systemic incentives. Direct force has the undesirable effect of shattering
that illusion and making it obvious the individual is no
longer participating in a voluntary association. Anyone
who witnesses this kind of enforcement on a consistent
basis just might start to question whether the country
really is still predicated on liberty and individual rights.

The application of force is also usually avoided by
foxes because they are bad at it. The judicious and effective use of violence is a skill like any other and it must
be properly honed in order to be reliably deployed. As
foxes become more confident in their station, they tend
to swap out the effective lions in their police and military for more compliant subordinates willing to play the
political game. A security force filled with ideological
adherents may be skilled at reinforcing propaganda, but
it tends to not be good at actual violence. If a government
wields violence correctly, it usually does not need to do it
very often, the consequences of disobedience being clear
for all to see. If, however, the police or military use violence and fail to accomplish their goal, the government
can lose legitimacy very quickly. A government without
the monopoly on force is no government at all, so if a
ruling elite cannot win a physical confrontation, it is best
to manufacture an excuse for why the confrontation is

unnecessary. Yes, that is a recipe for disaster, but fox-style elites who have to resort to violence on a regular basis are already living on borrowed time.

The creeping total state in America looks different from the Soviet Union, for example, because of the character of its leadership class. The slower, more methodical approach of foxes proved to be more flexible and resilient than the aggressive application of centralized control by lions. It also scaled far more reliably, which, as we will see, turned out to be a critical asset. This strategy proved more materially successful and benefited from a populace that believed the changes occurring around them were organic and voluntary.

There was another reason for the comparable stability of this system: the foxes' talent for managing large bureaucracies. It was a skill that was to make them indispensable to the emerging total state.

CHAPTER 6

The Origins of
the Managerial Elite

The story of the last two hundred years of human history is the story of the massification of society. The industrial revolution led to mass production, which demanded mass consumption and mass markets to properly utilize the scale at which production could now, and must now, occur. Regional communities, which had once operated with relative independence, needed to become interconnected through transit, finance, and communications if they were to tap into the abundance of industrialization. Materials, markets, and labor no longer needed to be located in close proximity due to the vast networks constructed to move them from one zone of optimal productivity to another. The managerial class is a product of the corporations and mass states deployed to oversee the coordination of this process.

As the advantages of scale and centralization became overwhelming, mass organizations came to dominate every aspect of life, including government, business, media, and education. Even social domains that would normally be more resistant to technocratic management and market forces, like religion, romantic relationships, and family formation, are now mediated by large bureaucratic institutions. Individuals are less and less likely to meet romantic partners through organic connections of family and church and more likely to have their dating experience mediated by large online companies promising to deploy advanced selection algorithms. Even churches are more likely to centralize and standardize operations, treating the winning of souls the same way a corporation treats a quarterly earnings report.

Bertrand de Jouvenel predicted that the ever-expanding state would dissolve these intermediate social spheres and bring them under its control amid its relentless quest for power. In many ways he was right, though he may have underestimated the degree to which the "private" sector of the economy would do the work of the state. The managerial class easily crosses the public/private barrier that has been so effectively constructed in the American psyche. The ability of managers to move from public government postings to private corporate positions while using the exact same language and skill set is key to the unification of the state and economy that managerialism ultimately requires.

As James Burnham explained in his book *The Managerial Revolution*, mass organizations are very complex and require large amounts of specific knowledge and technical expertise to operate. The ownership class of capitalists may have had the resources necessary to construct these leviathans, but they lacked the mastery of specialized functions required to steer the bureaucracy. This created demand for a class of workers educated in the art of managerial techniques and trained in their application. As the efficiency and scale of these organizations proved overwhelming, the mass bureaucracy became the default structure for every social institution. This naturally increased the demand for, and power of, those in the managerial class.

At the beginning of the industrial revolution, monied capitalists were the dominant class in the Western world. The expansion of trade, technological development, and the material surplus they had created allowed them to unseat the nobility. Absolute monarchies transitioned to constitutional monarchies and then to parliamentary democracies as power shifted from kings to merchants. Traditional structures, the competing social sphere de Jouvenel mentioned, had to that point limited the power of mass organizations. Earlier forms of social organization like feudalism relied heavily on regional divisions to protect the power of the ruling class. The logistical and technological complexity of central organization was simply impossible at many points in history and the regional autonomy of the feudal lord allowed him to defend his territory from princes or kings that would prefer more direct control. Capitalism had dissolved or weakened many of these institutions but still relied on some degree of regional autonomy to organize society and protect the power of the ownership class.

As the advantages of mass organization became too apparent to deny, traditional capitalists had to relax restrictions and allow large organizations to develop in order to keep pace with competitors. Capitalist elites were required to place their trust in managers who could oversee these organizations and integrate them into the existing power structure. At first, the relationship was one of employee to employer, but eventually a struggle for power inside these institutions would develop between the class that owned the capital and the class that managed the machine that capital had built.

The relationship was originally symbiotic as the managers were dependent on the capital provided by the owners. The capitalist, in turn, required the skills and technical expertise that the managerial class provided to defeat market competitors. The balance of power would slowly shift, however, as the interests of the capitalists and the managers diverged. Management is essentially the science of operating massive and complex organizations. Those in management positions become more powerful and essential to the organization as it grows and gains additional complexity. This means the main incentive of the managerial class is not to pursue the stated mission of the organization or deliver a particular service or a certain product or even necessarily to return the highest profit to owners or investors. Managers are incentivized to increase the size and complexity of their organization. This then grows their power and increases their share of benefits and profits.

With ownership and operation separated, the stated interests and the functional interests of the organization began to diverge, in small ways at first that became jarring over time. Understanding this conflict as purely economic is a mistake. The economic battle is only one front of a broader civilizational conflict in which managers challenge every institution that was a part of the capitalist social order. That includes moral and social codes, political structures, and religious organizations. Subversion of the previous institutions is key to the expansion of mass corporations, mass society, the mass state—and the managerial class.

Diversity, real diversity, which comes from localized institutions and regional culture, is the enemy of centralization. It must be broken down to promote the hegemony that allows for mass production, consumption, and media. Too much of the local creates moral particularism and cultural tastes, which are costly for the managerial state to adapt to and create drag on the system, making it far more difficult to create a uniform system of managerial control. It is much better to dissolve local diversity than to make allowances for its particularities.

The political theorist and commentator Samuel T. Francis, who updated and expanded upon James Burnham's work in his book *Leviathan and Its Enemies*, explained the need for homogenization:

"The corporation must promote the homogenization of society because of the nature of mass production and mass consumption. Mass production requires not only homogeneous goods and services produced by the same molds and processes, but also homogeneous consumers, who cannot vary in their tastes, values, and patterns of consumption and who must consume if the planning of the corporations is to be effective. The comparatively compact and differentiated institutions of the bourgeois order sustain its heterogeneity and constrain the consumption of mass-produced goods and services. Managerial capitalism must therefore articulate and sponsor an ideology of cosmopolitanism that asserts universal identities, values, and loyalties, challenges the differentiations of the bourgeois order, and rationalizes the process of homogenization. In the cosmopolitan view of man, family, local community, religious sect, social class, sexual and racial identity, and moral character are at best subordinate considerations and are regarded as artificial, repressive, and obsolete barriers to the fulfillment of human potential.

Cosmopolitanism thus rationalizes the adoption of the mass framework and collective disciplines that characterize the managerial regime and the homogenization of production and consumption through which the multinational organizations and economies of managerial capitalism operate."[1]

This homogenization dissolves the differences between corporation and state because the managerial elites assume control of each in essentially the same way. The technical knowledge required to direct these organizations, and the manipulation of public opinion needed to sell a product to consumers or a political project to voters, are increasingly similar. Every mass organization, be it a branch of the military or a fast food

---

1   Francis, *Leviathan and Its Enemies*, p.33.

restaurant, needs staff trained in public relations, supply chain logistics, technical support, and legal arbitration. The public or private nature of the organization makes no difference. In either case, the efficiency of bureaucracy relies on the ability of the managers to standardize the consumption, decision making, and work habits of those below them. Greater homogenization increases the likelihood that the organization can be effectively scaled up.

The almost total overlap of skills required to manage public and private bureaucracies is also facilitated by the standardization of credentialing mechanisms across all disciplines. Institutions of higher learning, once the domain of specialized academics and the children of the elite, truly began to assert their cultural dominance when they became government-subsidized finishing schools for the professional managerial class. The mass compulsory military service required during World War II led to the GI Bill. The wide availability of funding for higher education meant that more promising young adults from the lower and middle classes were able to afford college than at any time previously. The explosion of college degree holders into a market increasingly dominated by mass bureaucratic institutions resulted in an association of university credentials with the skills necessary to operate as a manager.

With the interests of the mass institutions now focused on the expansion of managerial power, those in the working and middle classes who desired social mobility focused increasingly on the attainment of college credentials. The incentives that drove the rapid growth of managerial positions in mass bureaucracies meant the opportunity to increase both status and wealth lay in the obtainment of managerial skills that could serve centralized power rather than privately owned capital that could liberate the holder from centralized power. The dream of social mobility through independence was replaced by a social mobility that was entirely dependent on utility to an interconnected network of mass organization.

While mass military service may have been the first vehicle for the growing state leviathan to subsidize the expansion of higher education, it would be far from the last. Social justice movements came to dominate the American political landscape and government programs like the Great Society and War On Poverty sought to raise communities that had been identified as "disadvantaged" to a higher standard of living and social standing. As college degrees became the credential du jour to enter the managerial class and achieve upward mobility, aid distributed to these communities increasingly came in the form of college scholarships and grants. Women, racial and sexual minorities, the disabled, and many others saw an explosion of funding for higher education with the explicit purpose of raising their members into managerial positions. An entire industry of nonprofit organizations grew up around the cause of providing aid to these communities, usually by absorbing funds from the government, and that aid always made funding for higher education a central goal. These large nonprofits were, of course, operated by bureaucracies full of college-educated managers. A self-exciting feedback loop was created to ensure the ever-expanding nature of the managerial class.

The state further accelerated this expansion by creating government-backed educational loans. By forgoing the option of discharge through bankruptcy, students with no income or collateral could secure loans well in excess of the value of a home. The resulting drastic increase and reliability of funding for college education meant that institutions of higher learning could greatly expand the range of their degree programs and the capacity of their campuses. Colleges themselves would now need large bureaucracies to oversee their training of students, who would in turn oversee large bureaucracies. The runaway nature of the cycle should be obvious.

As the college degree became ubiquitous at the upper levels of management, its cachet began to trickle down to lower levels too. If too many credentialed applicants were vying for top spots in an organization, then a few would naturally end up in the positions just below. The college credential would still ensure the candidate beat out everyone else in sub-elite management positions. This became the appeal of the degree. Their necessity eventually cascaded from the CEO of a grocery store chain all the way down to positions like general store manager, which had never required any higher education in the past.

The ubiquitous nature of the mandatory college credential across bureaucratic institutions, both public and private, meant that universities became the primary centers of enculturation for almost everyone who held any position of power. This was the genesis of the Cathedral. The shared formative experience of university education instilled not only a moral framework that informed the decision making of the new ruling class, but a shared understanding of how organizations should be structured and operated.

As we discussed briefly in chapter one, before becoming famous for his attacks on religion, Richard Dawkins created the meme, which described how ideas take on an evolutionary life of their own. Dawkins also suggested that, like viruses, memes could enter a human host and alter certain aspects of its behavior in order to replicate and spread itself. Just as genes undergo mutations that either prove advantageous and proliferate into the next generation or maladaptive and fatal to their host, ideas compete for the survival of the fittest. Entire interconnected networks of ideas can form into more sophisticated memeplexes in which memes support and reinforce each other. These memeplexes can create entire worldviews that shape how an individual and even a wider culture interact with any given information they encounter. Christianity, Islam, Stoicism, the scientific method, and progressivism would all qualify as memeplexes.

While universities were infecting entire generations with the progressive memeplex, they were also teaching them to trust in the bureaucratic process. It was the managerial elite that had produced the modern miracles of abundance and efficiency. It was entry into the managerial class through the college credential that offered a path to prosperity and social elevation. Truth did not come from bourgeois social authorities like family, church, and community, or even some noble aristocracy, but was defined exclusively via the quantifiable, predictable, and distributed authority of the bureaucratic process.

University-educated experts quickly became the only recognizable authority. The explosive growth of degree fields meant that academic language and managerial techniques could be brought to bear on every question. Corporations were obvious targets for this memeplex, but it quickly grew beyond the business world, revolutionizing every previously independent social sphere. The armed forces transitioned away from the leadership of grizzled veterans to organizations based on metrics, data, and corporate culture. Talk to any recently discharged veteran and he will tell you that the rapidly swelling staff of generals in the military has far more experience coordinating human resource seminars than with frontline combat. Parents stopped trusting the traditions of their communities and religions to raise their children, instead investing their faith in child psychologists and social workers. The bulk of the charity work that had once served as the cornerstone of churches' outreach was transferred to the massive and centralized welfare state. In every sphere, the managerial elite became the only validating mechanism for decision making.

With the hegemony of the progressive memeplex and ubiquity of the bureaucracy across every organization in society, the migration of managerial elites from one sector to another became effortless. The skills and social programming needed to operate within a university, news organization, corporation, nonprofit, and even law enforcement agency are all strikingly similar. A properly trained and credentialed manager can apply their techniques to any suitably homogenized set of subjects with little to no adaptation. It is, in fact, the desire for their skillset to be universalized across all organizations that drives the managerial class to homogenize all aspects of culture, consumption, and production.

With bureaucracy the only acceptable form for institutions to assume, the interaction between these institutions becomes its own valuable commodity.

This is why modern corporations regularly employ former government officials and bureaucratic functionaries for their expertise in interacting with the very agencies from which they came. Experience in law enforcement or intelligence can uniquely qualify someone to provide consultation to social media companies that regularly need to monitor and evaluate their platforms for credible threats. This is why the staffs of tech giants like Twitter, Google, and Facebook are littered with former FBI lead counsels and CIA analysts. The distinction between public and private dissolves as members of the managerial class flow effortlessly between both types of entities. Far from being a hindrance, service in a public institution and the insider knowledge acquired there becomes highly desirable for private corporations that must profitably interact with public entities on a regular basis. Public institutions seek out those with experience in private corporations for the same reason.

Sam Francis outlines how even the legal system has become an important battlefield in the war between the old bourgeois and the new managerial elites. Just as the capitalists used the principles of "rule of law" and "equality before the law" to limit and deconstruct the power of monarchs in the eighteenth and nineteenth centuries, the managerial elite seeks to shift the law towards results-based administrative procedure. Determinations in legal proceedings are increasingly dependent on experts who are part of the managerial class. The value of the law comes to rest on its ability to produce the economic and cultural changes desired by the social engineers.

Experts in fingerprinting, DNA, and gunshot analysis combine with psychologists and other therapeutic practitioners to manufacture plausible narratives on which the decisions of juries and judges hinge. Scientists of every stripe become key witnesses for all parties and their credentials mean their assertions can only be challenged by similarly credentialed experts inside the same managerial class. Determinations of law are increasingly transferred away from the traditional legal process and handed to panels of experts. Large bureaucratic entities craft contracts and formulate processes specifically to avoid contact with the legal system and ensure they are insulated from any non-managerial authority.

Managerial elites also create a moral narrative to justify their expansion of power through what author Paul Gottfried calls the therapeutic state. The therapeutic

state treats ills like crime, war, ignorance, and poverty
not as part of the human condition but as social pathologies. Experts identify these pathologies as the result of
autonomous social institutions, which just so happen to
be the cornerstones of bourgeois order. These competing spheres of social influence become the sources of ills
that can only be cured through the bureaucratic administration of scientifically developed therapies. Just as de
Jouvenel predicted, the total state uses this narrative as
a justification to collapse all competing institutions and
further centralize its power. This allows the state and
economy to merge in a more complete fashion. It pre-
pares the way for an attack on the remains of bourgeois
power. As Francis writes, "The fusion of the economy
with the state in the managerial regime enables the managers in the state sector to attack the economic centers
of the bourgeois power base by undermining the productivity and autonomy of the entrepreneurial firm. The
assault on entrepreneurial capitalism also weakens the
social institutions, political power, and ideologies of the
bourgeois elite by bringing hard property under attack
from the regulatory and interventionist policies of the
managerial state. But the state also undertakes political
reform and programs of social engineering that subvert
the bourgeois elite more directly. The ostensible purpose
of the political and social reforms is to ameliorate the
material conditions of the masses, oppressed by bourgeois selfishness and parochialism, and, indeed, this
purpose is often sincere in the minds of the managers
themselves. Whether sincere or not, however, the real

effect of managerial political and social reforms is to level bourgeois differentiations, to 'liberate' the masses from the tyranny of bourgeois or prescriptive institutions, and to homogenize the mass population and bring it under the discipline of the mass organizations. The alliance of mass and manager against the bourgeoisie constitutes the political basis of managerial Caesarism."[2]

The manager class simultaneously needs to drive popular opinion, collapse competing institutions, and justify the engineering of social tastes and behavior. Large-scale social engineering projects that increase compliance and generate efficiency by creating uniform consumption become increasingly important to the managers of the total state. To shore up its power, it must transform the populace into perfectly compliant subjects. And this it is well positioned to do.

---

2   Francis, *Leviathan and Its Enemies*, p.68.

CHAPTER 7

Engineering Subjects for the Total State

The total state seeks to maximize efficiency and stability by exerting control in every domain of life within its ever-expanding borders. In order to accomplish this, it deploys a network of managerial elites in both the public and private spheres who apply an approved system of standardized techniques. The goal of the managers is not just to create more efficiency, but to shape the organizations, workers, and consumers they manage so their techniques can be more uniformly applied. The more homogeneous large bureaucracies can make those they manage, the easier it is to predict outcomes and expand their power.

The problem is that human beings are radically different. Even if you find a way to engineer a workplace or educational institution where everyone is uniform, those within eventually leave those organizations and go home to families and communities, which can impact their performance when they return. If an employee is devoutly religious with six children at home, he may refuse to work twelve hours on a Sunday or object to the new line of puberty blockers the company health-care plan is rolling out. It may also be difficult to convince his wife to enter the workforce, lowering the cost of labor. Just as a champion sailboat racer seeks to remove every rough surface from his hull to reduce drag, a manager seeks to make every employee as compliant and friction-less as possible.

This means it is not enough for managers to enforce uniformity inside their organizations. The state must actively seek to shape the private and public lives of its citizens in order to homogenize influences that could introduce variance and instability. This level of engineer-ing requires a narrative superstructure that justifies inter-vention at almost every level of human interaction. The therapeutic approach to the human condition allows the state to mobilize social capital invested in concepts like science, mental health, and progress towards the goal of direct intervention in human development.

Man is deeply flawed. There is nothing new or shocking about this. It has been the subject of art, lit-erature, and religious belief for as long as those things have existed. It does not mean that both the moral and material conditions of man cannot or should not be improved, but it does mean accepting the difficult truth that there are limits to what can be done. Wise leaders used to temper the expectations of their followers when it came to improvement. The poor would always be with us; suffering and loss would always be a part of life. Many of the most disastrous episodes in history have occurred when zealots foresee the prospect of heaven on earth and become determined to use any means necessary to achieve it.

The scientific revolution led many to think the power of reason could be harnessed to alleviate aspects of the human condition that had once been considered unassailable. Progress had, of course, been made steadily across many domains of human endeavor, but the quantification and systematic optimization that the scientific mindset introduced seemed to fundamentally alter everything it came into contact with. Advancements in hard sciences came first, but applying such methods to fields like economics and politics had equally revolutionary results. It seemed that in almost every area of life, what had once been mysterious could be quantified, understood, and managed. The human condition thus might one day be altered or even completely controlled. Nothing had to be accepted; nothing was beyond reach. War, crime, poverty, inequality—these were no longer facts of life but engineering problems to be solved through the application of the scientific method and managerial techniques.

One process that illustrates this fundamental shift in approach is the medicalization of deviance. Every society has deviations from the norm that they view as negative. Traditionally, these have been understood as moral failings by the individual. Alcoholism, drug use, infidelity, obesity, and gambling have all been seen as vices, while indulgence in them was understood as sin, a moral failing. Those who repeatedly chose them were thus considered to have defects of character. The judgment of these vices and any attempt to understand and master them existed in the moral domain. The teachings of the church were the lens through which one viewed them and it was priests and other trusted moral leaders whom one consulted if one was to overcome their temptations.

Today, these issues are no longer seen as character flaws but medical conditions that can be ameliorated and even cured with the correct physiological or pharmaceutical course of treatment. Those suffering from these afflictions are not morally responsible for them, just as those suffering from cancer or dementia are not responsible for their condition. The transformation of moral failings into diagnosable medical conditions began with afflictions that could be reasonably associated with genetically heritable preferences, but it has since expanded to the vast majority of criminal and deviant behaviors in society. This transfer from the domain of the moral to the domain of the medical has been referred to by some sociologists as the medicalization of deviance.

What we must investigate is why the medicalization of deviance is such a persistent phenomenon in our society. Why is it so important to tie a large swath of behavior that was once socially unacceptable to medical diagnosis and treatment? What incentives are driving this trend? It should be said that there really have been significant advances in science that help us to better understand human behavior, and in some areas of mental health there have been important improvements based on these discoveries. But the blanket application of the medical approach to deviant behavior has been an unmitigated disaster.

Every society needs a narrative. Every civilization is built on a story about itself. Every people has a religion that binds it together, whether it recognizes it or not. Gilding that binding belief with the trappings of science and secularity does not mean you avoid this essential aspect of existence.

As we examined in chapter one, America and many other Western nations are guided by a decentralized atheistic theocracy of progressivism that Curtis Yarvin called the Cathedral. And like any religion, our atheistic theocracy needs a unifying narrative to explain the world as we find it, why it exists in a fallen state, and how we can work towards a better future. In an atheistic theocracy, professors and scientists replace the priestly caste. For the system to maintain legitimacy, all solutions to our social problems must come from this new order of priests. The faith of Western civilization has been vested in science, and science must therefore be able to resolve all social ills. If anything were to exist outside of its purview, if any of the critical issues we face required answers beyond what scientific disciplines could offer, then that would leave room for another authority or social sphere to speak on the topic, which could then compete for loyalty and resources. And if there is one thing no theocracy can tolerate, it's another authority providing answers.

Under the total state's model of behavior, humans are inherently good, with the possible exception of straight white Christian males. Rights originate from the individual's membership in the human collective. And because humanity is innately good, anything that deviates from that good must be explained as a defect caused by some force external to human nature. By removing or altering this external force, the naturally good function of man can be restored, like a robot in need of repair to return to working order. This means individuals must not be seen as immoral or sinful, but as medically ill. And like any patient who is ill, a course of treatment can be designed by an expert to heal the condition.

A materialistic worldview is another essential aspect of this atheistic theocracy. Science, by definition, cannot solve metaphysical problems. Everything must therefore exist on the material plane. Every aspect of the human condition must be the result of forces that are directly observable and quantifiable. This often requires a sleight of hand with the definition of science, or the creation of pseudoscientific disciplines, but these are acceptable compromises if they keep the narrative relatively coherent. Many areas that have acquired the label of "scientific discipline," especially the social sciences, are completely incapable of reliably reproducing the results of their studies. Despite this critical failure of scientific methodology, they continue to receive the moniker and prestige of expertise. By attaching the right jargon and peer-reviewed process, all of humanity can be brought under the purview of the managerial and scientific state.

Progress is one of the grand narratives of the total state. It promises that the managerial expertise of the ruling class will yield perpetual advancement in every area of society. Be it health care, civil rights, corporate profits, or technology, everything must advance and expand constantly. This also means all problems must be solvable. Suffering and tragedy cannot be understood as inevitable features of the human condition that can only be borne with grace and honor, as they have been in most traditional societies. People cannot have a fixed and tragic nature that they must learn to endure. Societies cannot understand their political systems as a series of tradeoffs where sacrifices must be made for the continuation of the civilization.

Under the total state, leaders are always progressing their citizens towards a more perfect future, which is always just around the corner. Like a donkey with a carrot dangled in front of it, our ruling class can never allow us to actually achieve our promised utopia or the whole system would stop moving. As we will see, it is control, not successful treatment, that drives the logic of the total state.

The medicalization of deviance is far from a neutral process. It picks political winners and losers even as it attempts to relocate the human condition entirely within the medical domain. A man who cheats on his spouse is not an adulterer; he is a sex addict whose condition requires understanding, therapy, and rehabilitation. If someone cannot hold down a job or is spending all of their family's money on drugs, they are an addict, and should not feel shame or blame but be understood as a victim with a genetic predisposition towards this behavior. A scientifically derived treatment administered by the managerial class will return the subject back to their natural state of human perfection.

In the case of sexual preference, the medicalization of deviance can even remove the need for treatment entirely. People are born with their sexual preference and there is simply nothing to fix. In some cases, these predispositions are held up as something to be celebrated with festivals and parades. This rationalization would seem to clash with the total state's newest obsession, transgenderism, where biological realities that are also determined by genetics can and must be surgically and chemically altered. So far this conflict of rationales has been held at bay by simply screaming "bigot!" at any-one who points out the obvious. This is a sloppy use of power on the part of the total state and we will discuss why it signals weakness in a later chapter.

The narrative of medicalization is of course riddled with politically convenient logical inconsistencies. If genetic determination is an acceptable justification for sexual preference, why would it not be the same for the in-group preference now commonly referred to as rac-ism? There is no logically consistent answer, but this is easily stepped over by the experts. While all behaviors will be medicalized, some are to be eradicated, some are to be tolerated, and some are even to be venerated. Why does genetic determination justify some behaviors while requiring the eradication of others? Only the experts are qualified to decide, and the new priestly caste will always favor the political priorities of the total state.

There is currently an effort afoot to relabel pedophiles as "minor attracted persons" who are victims of their own biology. Yet simultaneously there is an attack on the natural biological preference of men for physically fit and attractive mates. One genetic preference makes you a misogynist; the other makes you a victim worthy of sympathy. It does not take a rocket scientist to see which group the state is seeking to target for punishment and which it is seeking to rehabilitate and normalize through medicalization.

The process of medicalization quickly bleeds over into the political realm. Cable news shows are flooded with medical experts who diagnose their political opponents with mental illness or limited cognitive capacity. In the total state, there can be no competing moral values, no cultural differences, no alternative conclusions. The regime's experts have already determined what the correct conclusions are. Anyone disagreeing with those conclusions cannot have arrived at their position through any kind of valid reasoning. Disagreement is a clear indication of mental illness, and not one of the approved mental illnesses that deserves sympathy and understanding, but one of the dangerous mental illnesses that makes the dissident evil and a social pariah. The wrongthinkers are not rational individuals with valid concerns; they are racists, sexists, bigots who can be safely discarded.

Medicalization is useful to the total state not just for marginalizing their opponents but also for rationalizing their persecution. No modern liberal democracy would send their dissidents to a concentration camp; that would be barbaric. Enlightened progressive leaders will instead seek to rehabilitate. The reeducation camps will be modern and scientific, using the latest physiological treatments and best medications to return the mind of the wrongthinker to its proper function. They are not crushing dissent; they are helping the mentally ill. They are not tyrannically controlling thought and behavior; they are saving the victims of a disease. This is why we see the fervent advance of the medicalization of deviance in all areas of our society. It's a materialistic theology that undergirds the narrative put forward by our ruling class. It justifies the actions of the rulers to a populace that might otherwise ask uncomfortable questions.

The state therefore adopts a therapeutic culture that enables the constant intrusion of managerial professionals to administer "scientifically" developed courses of treatment to reduce undesirable thoughts, attitudes, preferences, and behavior. The raising of a child, a task that for many thousands of years fell to his parents, extended family members, and the organic community in which they existed, now requires the intervention of experts at every moment. Medical doctors are, of course, a regular feature of the child's life, but increasingly parents are encouraged to discard the timeless practices passed down through their family or religion and instead consult the opinions of credentialed experts when it comes to discipline, diet, socialization, and mental health. Child therapy replaces Sunday school and carefully curated playdates replace meeting the kids next door for a game of pickup football.

The total state's management of children is most effectively achieved through compulsory state-funded education. The student is managed at all times by credentialed experts, with every aspect of their day planned through the constant application of managerial techniques. All issues of discipline are settled through increasingly therapeutic models of resolution. At every stage, undesirable prejudices and moral particularities are stripped away through the application of therapeutic courses of behavioral modification.

Mothers and fathers who do not heed the advice of a state-appointed manager can be stripped of their parental rights. If a teacher, social worker, or guidance counselor manages to convince a child that they are a transexual, a parent must tread with extreme caution. Any rejection of the diagnosis or course of treatment can be used as evidence of neglect or even abuse. Political wrongthink can indicate a parent's resistance to managerial authority and demonstrate just how unfit they are to oversee the development of their own child.

The author C.S. Lewis predicted this managerial process in his prophetic book *The Abolition Of Man*, which he wrote in the 1940s. Lewis begins by describing a common educational text of his time that he calls The Green Book and whose authors he dubs Gaius and Titius. After taking the reader through some of its passages, he points out that while some of them do stir the human soul, the accompanying questions which the students are required to answer do exactly the opposite. After each passage, the authors make sure to undermine its spirit. A reading that was originally intended to communicate the sublime beauty and wonder of nature is characterized by The Green Book's authors as overly emotional and subjective.

Criticism and skepticism of anything showing organic emotion, passion, feeling, or romance is constantly encouraged. According to Lewis, the student is just reading the book as part of their grammar lesson, yet while they're learning very little about the English language or literature, they're being taught how they should approach the world. Every commentary, every question posed to the child is slowly cutting away a piece of their soul, making sure they grow skeptical of metaphysically animating human traits like heroism, passion, and wonder. The only value reinforced is the idea of cold and objective analysis.

It is critical for the student to debunk and embarrass anyone who would show the wrong kind of passion or emotion. The overseers will instill many deeply emotional prejudices into the student, but they will be the preferences desired by the total state for optimal application of managerial techniques. Those prejudices will be treated as the null hypothesis, the rational default against which all other articulations of truth and aesthetic preferences must be judged.

The intellectuals who authored The Green Book would like to give the impression they are preparing students to be cold and rational evaluators without any particular bias or worldview, but of course this is not the case. These educators are trying to reproduce in children the thought process preferred by those who rely on the application of managerial techniques. While this bias toward materialism and bloodless rationality benefits the total state, the children are left a little less human for the experience.

As Lewis writes, "The operation of The Green Book and its kind is to produce what may be called Men without Chests. It is an outrage that they should be commonly spoken of as intellectuals. This gives them the chance to say that he who attacks them attacks Intelligence. It is not so. They are not distinguished from other men by any unusual skill in finding truth nor any virginal ardor to pursue her. Indeed it would be strange if they were: a persevering devotion to truth, a nice sense of intellectual honor, cannot be long maintained without the aid of a sentiment which Gaius and Titius could debunk as easily as any other. It is not excess of thought but defect of fertile and generous emotion that marks them out. Their heads are no bigger than the ordinary: it is the atrophy of the chest beneath that makes them seem so.

"And all the time—such is the tragicomedy of our situation—we continue to clamor for those very qualities we are rendering impossible. You can hardly open a periodical without coming across the statement that what our civilization needs is more 'drive' or dynamism, or self-sacrifice or 'creativity.' In a sort of ghastly simplicity we remove the organ and demand the function. We make men without chests and expect of them virtue and enterprise. We laugh at honor and are shocked to

find traitors in our midst. We castrate and bid the geld-
ings be fruitful."[1]

Lewis was warning all the way back in the 1940s
that humanity was heading down a very dangerous path.
Abolishing sincerity, beauty, and passion by materializing
every aspect of human existence has serious consequences.

"We reduce things to mere nature in order that we
may 'conquer' them," Lewis continues. "We are always
conquering nature because 'nature' is the name for what
we have, to some extent, conquered. The price of conquest is to treat a thing as mere nature. Every conquest
over nature increases her domain. The stars do not
become nature till we can weigh and measure them: the
soul does not become nature till we can psychoanalyze
her. The wresting of powers from nature is also the sur-
rendering of things to nature. As long as this process
stops short of the final stage we may well hold that the
gain outweighs the loss. But as soon as we take the final
step of reducing our own species to the level of mere
nature, the whole process is stultified, for this time the
being who stood to gain and the being who has been
sacrificed are one and the same."[2]

Lewis made a prediction that proved to be very accu-
rate with regard to the total state. He explained that
once a generation truly masters human nature, once they
understand how to strip man of the sacred and reduce
him to a material object, mere inputs and outputs that

---

1   Lewis, *The Abolition of Man*, p.83.
2   Lewis, *The Abolition of Man*, p.35.

can be manipulated and engineered, then that generation will become the last that is truly human. By controlling and reshaping man from the ground up, Lewis predicts that social engineers will eventually abolish man and create a shadow of humanity that is easier to manage. This drone-like species would be crippled from the start, incapable of the heights and depths of its ancestors.

While Lewis may not have had access to our linguistic frame of bureaucratic managerialism, he recognized the process by which the total state would increase its capacity to centralize control. A thoroughly secularized therapeutic culture would create the narrative justification for constant state intervention through the bureaucratic application of scientifically developed courses of treatment. By stripping away the natural human preference for particular cultures, religions, moral systems, and aesthetics, social engineers can create subjects that are far easier to manage. This dehumanization, this abolition of man, was necessary if the total state was to continue its centralization of control.

CHAPTER 8

Managed Dehumanization and the Global State

In 1941, James Burnham published his book *The Managerial Revolution* in an attempt to explain the fundamental transformation that the world around him was undergoing. To most observers, it appeared that communism, fascism, and liberal democracy were the three major systems competing for supremacy on the world stage. Burnham noted, however, that these three systems shared one trait: a class of highly specialized managers operating a network of large bureaucracies with the goal of standardizing and planning their societies from the top down. Initially, this was easier to observe in the hard totalitarian states that existed under fascism or communism, where official organs dictated social and economic behavior. The tight grip of the managers in those societies drove them to collapse, while in the liberal West managers used a gradual approach that proved more resilient.

This more gradual approach allowed the citizens of liberal democracies to believe they had escaped the fate of other nations that had succumbed to suffocating bureaucracy. While the comforting notions of the free market and social tolerance made Americans feel victorious as the last remnants of the Soviet Union collapsed, the soft managerial elite that dominated the West was able to bring more and more aspects of society under their control. Government agencies, corporations, media outlets, and educational institutions increasingly seemed to act with one voice and one agenda, instead of behaving as the separate, self-interested actors described by classical liberalism. With the incredible degree of coordination our elites demonstrated during the 2020 elections and pandemic lockdowns, this truth has become much easier for the average American to observe.

The cunning manipulation of the foxes who operated the managerial infrastructure in liberal democracies has outlasted the nakedly authoritarian approach of their more lion-ish competitors. Social engineering through the soft but firm manipulation of institutions that were presented as culturally neutral allowed the total state to mold the populace into more compliant subjects without triggering the pushback that direct force usually engenders. Stripped of the intermediate social spheres that sheltered them from the totalizing state, people came to see themselves as liberated individuals making selections in a free and open market. Few thought to ask who had engineered the choices inside that market and why those selections reliably seemed to favor the power of the state.

While the expansion of individual choice through liberation from traditional social bonds was celebrated, the average citizen became more reliant on the media for his sense of identity and more reliant on the state for his day-to-day needs. Despite the theoretical check on power that the electorate was supposed to represent, the expansion of the franchise always correlated with an increase, not a decrease, in the size and scope of the government. The total state came to secure reliably engineered outcomes through the democratic process—not necessarily by stealing elections outright but through the manipulation of information and voter preferences. The distributed theocratic oligarchy of liberal democracy proved a far more resilient method of establishing totalitarian control than the hard and obvious centralizing powers in other managerial regimes.

In order to condition subjects through managerial techniques, the state needs to deracinate and dehumanize the individual. Human identity is not an individual construction; it's assembled through dependencies and duties in relation to the surrounding community. When we are young, our identity is formed by our relationship with our parents and extended family. As we reach adolescence, a wider network of cultural institutions gains influence. In adulthood, we take on additional duties that bind us to others who are dependent on our protection, provision, and guidance. It's this social fabric that holds a community together and gives the individual his identity.

Human identity is not forged through a set of absolute freedoms or rights; it's found in the limitations that culture and circumstance impose on the individual. It is the dependence on and duty to local and regional institutions that create the true manifestation of cultural diversity. These idiosyncrasies are what allow for different varieties of cuisine, dress, and architecture. The varying regional pressures on courtship, habitation, and familial succession shape very different understandings of family and community. Even in widespread faiths like Christianity and Islam, regional differences can have a dramatic impact on ritual, worship, and the relationship between church and state. Human identity is thus shaped far more dramatically by what the individual is not than what he is free to become.

This is why individual liberation is a consistent theme of the total state. Instead of seizing authority through direct force, the managerial elite found it much easier to expand their power by first assuming the duties that once belonged to opposing social spheres like family and church, and then gradually usurping the power that naturally flows from that dependence. The individual felt increasingly liberated from the heavy burden of care for relatives, the education of children, and the duty to maintain community. All the while, he barely noticed that his culture was slowly atrophying and his identity, once defined by a tight web of social bonds, was fading away.

Instead, the total state assured its managed subjects that identity was like a seasonal fashion, something that could be tried on when it suited the individual and then discarded before the next exciting round of consumption. The very factors that had once shaped and defined essential aspects of being were now disposable products that could be switched out with startling frivolity. Such hedonism served to make him increasingly dependent on the state. In very short order, he was conditioned to find the rearing of children and the maintenance of social institutions as insurmountable tasks that required the regular intervention of the state and the expertise of its managers.

Such deculturation and dehumanization allows the total state to bring its citizens under its own power by abolishing all competing entities that could create rival dependences. It is for this reason that the managerial class must attack all remnants of bourgeois independence that could serve to shelter holdouts from their all-consuming advance.

Hard property like housing and land, anything that could provide stability and opportunity, becomes a problem. There is a reason the World Economic Forum has made "You will own nothing and you will be happy" its unapologetic slogan. The ideal system is one in which every aspect of the subject's life is rented from massive entities, ensuring no stability can ever be achieved. Similarly, independent employment and entrepreneurship is a threat to the total dependence demanded by the managerial formula. Everyone who is allowed to earn a living apart from the mass bureaucracy is a threat.

This is why the eradication of the American middle class is a top priority for the total state. In the past, the managers may have expanded their influence due to the vast consumption enabled by a booming middle class, but now the independence and stability that have been generated by such wealth have become a threat to their power.

Originally, the American middle class was defined by the autonomy it achieved through the ownership of private property. Middle-class families owned their own land, their own homes, their own cars, and very often their own independent businesses. The father could usually earn enough on one income, allowing the mother to homeschool her children or at least be heavily involved in their rearing and education, removing any dependence on government-subsidized childcare. Churches, civic organizations, mutual aid societies, and fraternal organizations created a social fabric separate from the systems of the state. Regional identities and particularities could be sheltered from managerial homogenization.

Today, the idea of the middle class has changed. It no longer signifies having a degree of independence achieved through material wellbeing but is simply a comfortable income bracket capable of selecting from a wider variety of subscription services. The traditional twenty-year home mortgage was first extended to thirty years, and now families are looking at forty-year-plus intergenerational loans in order to afford a home. Large investment capital and overseas firms intentionally buy up starter homes that would have allowed young families to become independent and convert them to mass corporate rental holdings. An entire generation has been intentionally priced out of home ownership with the goal of conditioning families to rent for their entire lives.

Cars have undergone a similar mentality shift as loan durations stretch from two years to five or more. Leases, under which the driver never owns his car, have become the norm and practice. Trading in a car for another round of debt has become widely accepted behavior.

The physical ownership of media has also become a thing of the past as Americans have embraced the live streaming of music, television, and video games. The home bookshelf now exists as subscriptions to services like Audible. Companies can and do censor their content in real time to adjust for "cultural sensitivities" manufactured by the total state.

Middle-class status is thus no longer signified by independence but by being able to afford subscriptions to Netflix, Hulu, and HBO Max. All of these services absorb surplus income while adjusting their content curation to censor movies and shows deemed objectionable by the state. Streaming media also relentlessly produces thinly veiled propaganda for their consumers, manufacturing the illusion of limitless options while drowning the watcher in an ocean of cultural hegemony.

Samuel Francis notes that this reconstruction of the middle class has made historical American values seem irrelevant to those living under the new managerial regime. It's allowed the total state to create a world in which alternatives to its power seem increasingly impossible.

Francis writes, "The dematerialization of property and the replacement of the entrepreneurial firm as the dominant form of economic organization by the mass corporations and unions under managerial control eroded both the economic power base of the bourgeois elite as well as the institutional roots of the bourgeois worldview. The reorganization of the population from the particularized, localized, private, and family and community centered institutions of the bourgeois order into the massive, anonymous, highly mobile, homogenized, and routinized disciplines of the managerial regime subverted the bourgeois worldview and the ideologies based on it by rendering its ideas and values irrelevant to the actual life-styles of post-bourgeois groups. The proletarianization of the post-bourgeois social formations thus consists not only in the disappearance of economic and social autonomy through the erosion of hard property and independent ownership but also in the cultural dispossession involved in the deracinating transformation provoked by the revolution of mass and scale and the dominance of managerial elites."[1]

Yet the total state's project of mass engineering does not stop at its own nation's borders. As we have seen, managerial organizations expand their power by bringing the largest possible number of resources, both human and material, under the control of their bureaucratic processes. Once the managerial class has obtained sufficient mastery over its original host country, the national border comes to feel like an artificial barrier to continued expansion.

---

1   Francis, *Leviathan and Its Enemies*, p.573.

The post-colonial West has been laying the groundwork for this expansion for some time. It did not take long for governments to realize that formal colonization was an outdated and inefficient political technology. Traditional colonies are a messy and clumsy way of extracting resources and creating hegemony; they also clash with the Western narrative of democracy and liberation. Instead of officially conquering other nations, it is far better to ensure they are run by local governments that are completely aligned with the West's interests. The themes of modernization and human rights are particularly useful in this new form of cultural conquest.

Modernization is its own very powerful argument. Washing machines, indoor plumbing, medical care, and consistent calorie counts are a very compelling reason to seek alliance with the West. Of course, Western liberal democracies prefer to work with other liberal democracies and aid is usually dependent on adopting this governmental form. Nations that did not reach this level of development on their own will also need to import an expert class to implement modernization and train its own managerial class to maintain it. Electrical grids, communication networks, highway systems, and the distribution of clean water are no small feats, and their rapid deployment is best handled by those trained in the management of mass institutions. That managerial class naturally works hand-in-hand with the one that spawned it. The newly modernized nations are also heavily dependent on trade with their benefactors as well as loans held by international managerial organizations.

Non-governmental organizations play a key part as well in keeping newly modernized nations dependent on the managerial framework.

While the pull of modernization is enough for most countries, holdouts can be persuaded through a number of different means. Gunboat diplomacy may have opened up nations like China and Japan, but our current fox-style elites are far more comfortable with economic and cultural subversion. Color revolutions have become the preferred tool for dealing with nations that have not yet embraced democracy, or with democracies that have not proven sufficiently compliant. The ubiquitous nature of Western media means only the most isolated communities have been spared from relentless propagandizing about human rights. Those seeking cultural ascendancy in Romania or Ukraine can be found complaining about abortion restrictions or limitations on trans rights in Alabama. People like this are ripe for cultural manipulation and can easily be used to disrupt the internal function of a resistant government.

While economic and cultural manipulation are the preferred vectors of attack, the managerial regime can fall back on brute force when necessary. Vastly superior air coverage, state of the art drone technology, and naval carrier groups can go a long way toward compelling a "rogue state" to fall in line. The increased reliance on complex technology and the ideological reconfiguration of Western militaries has, however, lessened the effectiveness of this once overwhelming force. One need only look at recent embarrassments like the American withdrawal from Afghanistan after decades of nation building to see that fox-like managers struggle to wield force effectively when the situation demands it.

Whether they are brought there by material improvements, cultural subversion, or brute force, modernized countries quickly become dependent on the managerial apparatus. Democratically elected political leaders rely on the persuasion of mass media to maintain power. Their economies depend on the material surplus generated by mass production. Their nation is usually secured by a web of international mutual defense treaties generated by the economically intertwined network of liberal democracies. The new regimes that came to power through the assistance of the wider West owe their positions not to their own people but to the material improvements, cultural control, and military protection granted to their ruling elites by the managerial apparatus. Most of their rulers are well aware of this fact, and those who forget are quickly made an example of through economic sanctions, mass media campaigns, and occasionally brute military force.

After the first wave of managers is imported into a modernized nation, subsequent generations can be trained at Western educational institutions. The rulers might be fellow countrymen by birth, but they will gain their status by acquiring managerial skills and connections in the West. Just as universities served to create a shared moral and cultural framework for the managerial class in America, these newly minted international elites will have more in common with other Western elites than they will with their fellow citizens. Whatever their original tongue, they will all speak the same language when it comes to gaining and maintaining power. An international class of elites with a similar culture and set of interests thus emerges.

Newly formed modern democracies may be reliant on the West for their power, but that relationship eventually transitions to interdependence. The Western managerial apparatus expands its operation into these satellite nations, taking advantage of cheaper labor and a vast expansion of mass consumption in new markets. An increasing number of highly specialized tasks are outsourced and sophisticated networks are created to coordinate the logistics of transportation, communication, and assembly required to extract the maximum efficiency and profit. Managerial techniques make this coordination possible, but they are stretched to their limits, relying on the regular function of bureaucratic networks established overseas in order to complete even the most basic tasks of production. With each expansion, the level of complexity grows, creating ever more demand for managerial expertise. The feedback loop grows even tighter.

The international expansion of mass bureaucracy opens up vast reserves of new power to the managerial elite, but it also comes with a new set of challenges. If bureaucratic organizations are to operate internationally, they must generate efficiency through the standardization of managerial techniques, just as they did inside their nations of origin. This means the workers, students, consumers, and voters under their rule must become culturally homogenous so their actions are predictable and can be reliably managed. Bringing billions of people from wildly diverse backgrounds with competing moral and cultural priorities under the same network of mass organizations would be impossible. Mass production and mass consumption require absolute regularity to generate their efficiency and become useless if creation and consumption are disrupted at unpredictable intervals.

For the ever-expanding network of managerial bureaucracy to spread profitably into new regions, it must successfully homogenize culture. It is not enough for a culture to become uniform inside a nation; it must become uniform across the entire international network. The conversion of nations into liberal democracies assists in this process. Democratic elites must introduce mass media, bureaucratic organization, and therapeutic amelioration if they are to achieve the kind of social engineering that is required to maintain power under a system of popular sovereignty. New democratic leaders in foreign countries thus benefit greatly from connecting their subjects to the global network of managers already established by the West. Mass media begins its work, and McDonald's, Starbucks, and Apple stores soon follow.

The particulars and history of the nation are slowly worn away as a tide of foreign culture flows in. International organizations become major employers as well as cultural staples and grow in importance until they are so integral to the operation of the country that no one can imagine how they ever got along without them. Managers and personnel flow over borders as naturally as the goods those organizations produce. The very idea that the people differ in any significant way from those of any other country slowly disappears. No group has claim to any given nation because all nations are now part of the mass managerial network. The managerial elite develop international class interests because their interdependent networks make the nation itself an interchangeable unit. Managing a government is seen as no different than running an international corporation or a non-governmental organization. All these entities feature similar bureaucratic structures and managers have an easy time moving between them.

This global managerial class naturally gives rise to international organizations designed to coordinate their actions and act in their interests. Some, like NATO, may start as a military or trade alliance. Others, like the International Monetary Fund and World Bank, may claim to fight poverty. But the overriding purpose quickly becomes the establishment and defense of mass managerial bureaucracies. The World Economic Forum more or less does this explicitly, championing the abolition of hard property, destruction of national borders, and mass social engineering. The notion of the Open Society, famously promoted by George Soros, casts humanity as one interchangeable mass that, once properly conditioned, can be ruled through one unified system. These organizations always emphasize problems of an international scale. Global warming, pandemic response, and world overpopulation are all issues that are too large for any one nation to address on its own. By focusing on large and abstract issues, the managerial elite can locate their decision-making centers well outside of the nation itself. This makes it almost impossible for the citizens of that nation to hold real power accountable even as they continue to participate in the democratic process.

Some countries, like China, understand that joining this liberal democratic managerial system means an abdication of sovereignty, and decide the benefits of self-determination outweigh the costs of being excluded. China and other nations are working to create their own bloc of international networks in order to resist the Western attempt at globalization. Always and everywhere, power seeks to centralize. Once the total state has captured all the power inside its borders, it will seek to expand those borders, and only another global leviathan can hope to resist its advance.

CHAPTER 9

Cthulhu and the Total State

The political theorist Curtis Yarvin said, "Cthulhu swims slowly, but he always swims to the left."

When we look at the total state and the managerial elite, it is difficult to deny that history seems to have taken a decidedly left-wing bent. Even the currently fashionable label given to leftists, progressives, denotes a historic inevitability to the advancement of their cause. But why would the massification of society and the dominance of the managerial elite result in a leftward political drift? The answer lies in the scale of modern civilization and the conflicting incentives that arise inside complex organizations.

The historian and poet Robert Conquest developed three laws of politics during his time as an academic lecturer:

1. Everyone is conservative about what he knows best.
2. Any organization not explicitly and constitutionally right-wing will sooner or later become left-wing.

3. The behavior of any bureaucratic organization can best be understood by assuming that it is controlled by a secret cabal of its enemies.

These laws can help us understand how individuals and institutions behave as civilizations expand and ultimately as the total state is formed.

Institutions are founded by either a single individual or a small group that has a specific vision in mind. Whether it be a tribe, government, church, or corporation, the mission of the organization is shaped early on by those who are deeply invested in its wellbeing and the people it serves. This is where Conquest's first law comes in: we are all conservative about the things we know best. A real estate mogul will take risks with a distant investment property that he would never take with the home where his children lay their heads. A banker will make a predatory high-interest loan to a stranger that he would not make to a friend. A politician is far more likely to allow the early release of criminals in a neighborhood whose streets he does not have to walk after dark.

This may seem obvious, but it's important to remember when we are talking about the scale of civilization. People are more conservative when they care about the things their decisions impact, when they are more likely to directly feel the costs of the risks they take. The author Nassim Nicholas Taleb calls this phenomenon "having skin in the game." Institutions usually have the clearest vision of their purpose at their founding because they're still small enough to stay focused on why they were created. They haven't yet acquired the levels of complexity that cause them to drift.

If most organizations start with a conservative focus on their mission, why would they inevitably become left-wing? Many progressives would answer that this is simply because what they believe is morally correct, that the arrow of history truly does favor leftism, and that this is the predictable result. While that's a very convenient narrative for those on the Left, I think it's best to be skeptical of their claims of manifest destiny. Instead we can use Conquest's Second Law to look inside the nature of human organization.

Remember, when a company or an organization is created, it is usually founded by a single visionary individual or group. The drive of that founder grants a unifying will that binds everyone involved and moves them towards the organization's goal. There are drawbacks to this arrangement, to be sure. A single individual can drive an organization to failure just as easily as success. But in their founding moments, most forms of social organization benefit from the decisive actions made possible by forging ahead towards one clear goal.

We can see this play out in Hollywood. Most people recognize that truly great movies are created by imaginative and highly dedicated directors. Films that are subject to significant interference from studio executives, those that are made by committee, almost uniformly become creative disasters. There is nothing about full directorial control that guarantees a great movie, and plenty of filmmakers create mediocre films. But film-making by committee all but guarantees a mediocre film. While many look forward to the next Martin Scorsese or Christopher Nolan movie, no one is excited to see the thirty-seventh comic book franchise sequel that has been assembled with the input of twenty different Disney studio executives.

It's a problem that's captured by sayings like "Too many cooks spoil the pot" and "Too many chiefs, not enough Indians." People inherently understand there is something about the creative process that is destroyed by the distribution of responsibility and the implementation of a bureaucratic structure. So it is that as bureaucracy creeps in, an organization also experiences mission creep. And once some aspect of the mission is up for debate, individual actors sense the chance to secure power within the organization for themselves. This leads to institutional drift and, eventually, decline. As different factions pull in different directions, organizations, institutions, civilizations, and, yes, even movies fall apart. Entropy comes for us all in the end.

Creating a well-functioning society is difficult, so when you have one it becomes incredibly important to protect it. That means encoding the lessons your ancestors learned into something that can transmit their knowledge to future generations so they do not need to relearn those lessons at great cost. This is the main purpose of tradition, passing down wisdom and identity from generation to generation, but this process is never perfect. Over time, every civilization loses part of its traditional identity because its people forget the costs that were paid to learn these lessons. They forget why they practiced the tradition in the first place and what life was like before barriers were put in place.

Competing factions start asking, "Do we really need this restriction? Do we really need that ritual behavior?" Slowly but surely traditions are worn away until the civilization loses what made it great in the first place and collapses. Families, institutions, religions, buildings, gardens, and civilizations eventually fall into decay and disrepair if they are not actively maintained. Entropy is an omnipresent force, and it applies to social organizations just as it applies to anything else in the universe.

Chaos, not order, is the natural state of the world, and chaos will always wear away at the structures of civilization. This is why it feels like history is moving to the left, why organizations that are not actively maintained drift left over time. Cthulhu is the process of civilizational entropy from which we can never escape.

In his essay "The Dark Enlightenment," the philosopher Nick Land expands on this idea while exploring dialectics and the role they play in the entropic process. Land claims the Left thrives on dialectics while the Right perishes by them, and that an integrative public debate always moves things to the left:

"The dialectic begins with political agitation, and extends no further than its practical, antagonistic, factional and coalitional 'logic'. It is the 'superstructure' for itself, or against natural limitation, practically appropriating the political sphere in its broadest graspable extension as a platform for social domination. Everywhere that there is argument, there is an unresolved opportunity to rule.

The Cathedral incarnates these lessons. It has no need to espouse Leninism, or operational communist dialectics, because it recognizes nothing else. There is scarcely a fragment of the social 'superstructure' that has escaped dialectical reconstruction, through articulate antagonism, polarization, binary structuring, and reversal. Within the academy, the media, even the fine arts, political super-saturation has prevailed, identifying even the most minuscule elements of apprehension with conflictual 'social critique' and egalitarian teleology. Communism is the universal implication. More dialectics is more politics, and more politics means 'progress' —or social migration to the left."[2]

Once the core values of a social organization are up for debate, they are over. Once the foundational axioms of an organization have entered the realm of open discussion, it will always and inevitably move to the left. Any organization that has not secured its foundation against this dialectical erosion will fall to the relentless forces of entropy. Anyone who is not defending, maintaining, and gatekeeping the things they love and care about will watch them decay and eventually be destroyed. Even with those efforts, every organization will eventually fall. Founding, growth, collapse, and rebirth are all part of the historical cycle and nothing ever truly escapes

---

2   Land, *The Dark Enlightenment*, p. 55–56.

them. No institution can maintain neutrality or stay stationary, because any institution that is not explicitly right-wing (actively maintaining and defending its core mission) will inevitably become left-wing.

The nature of bureaucratic structures was thus critical to the rise of the total state. Conquest's third law speaks further to the way those structures behave as civilization massifies. As an organization grows, it must increase in complexity. The shared vision of the organization, which was first communicated by its dynamic founding members, must be transmitted into standards and procedures that can be reliably replicated by a large number of managers. For a social organization to increase its load-bearing capacity, it must eventually shift from serving the individual needs of its customers or citizens and instead shape their needs to serve the organization. Once the organization has birthed a bureaucracy that can prioritize its own needs over those it was designed to serve, a clear split develops in the incentive structure, and that split only widens over time.

The owner or founder of an organization is primarily concerned with its success, but this is not the primary interest of the manager. The manager is simply one of many bureaucrats, and while he may be impacted by the overall success or failure of the organization, his primary concern is his own position. As the scale of the organization grows, it creates departments that specialize in different functions. With each partition, the organization grows increasingly complex and abstract as each department becomes more focused on its own

specialization than on the overall success of the institution itself. Managers become motivated by the accu-
mulation of power and prestige inside this bureaucratic
ecosystem.

As the organization grows and becomes more influen-
tial, this power struggle only intensifies. For the individual managers, the internal political game becomes more
important than the original mission of the organization
or the people it serves. Managers need opportunities to
obtain power, and as Land explains, disagreement provides a chance to rule. Harmony and consensus are of no
use to the ambitious manager: he must sow discord and
leverage that factionalism for his own gain.

Amid this internecine warfare, managers drive their
organizations to the left because this is the direction of
division and therefore power. If, to take one example,
men are seen as an established sex and can never become
women, there is no power to be gained from that set fact.
Undebatable axioms maintain existing power structures,
as they are inherently conservative in nature. But if men
suddenly *can* become women, now there is an opportunity for dialectic, polarization, and factionalism. The
disagreement creates internal politics, allows managers
to secure power, and drives the organization leftward.

In the business world, this phenomenon is often
called the principle-agent problem. When the interests
of the individual taking an action are no longer aligned
with the interests of the person or group who will bear
the cost of that action, disaster usually follows. This
is why every bureaucracy eventually cannibalizes the

organization it was built to serve. Eventually, the incentives for managers are so desperately out of line with the interests of the institution that it looks like it is being run by a cabal of its enemies.

Bud Light is a brand built almost entirely on its popularity among the working class and red-state Americans. It is the default beer of backyard barbeques, football games, and country music concerts. No trendy urbanite or socially conscious activist would be caught dead drinking Bud Light. Anheuser-Busch is perfectly aware of this dynamic and has made billions of dollars by leaning into this image. Their advertisements are not aimed at progressive college professors or *New York Times* readers. They are aimed squarely at Joe Sixpack.

Despite this, and despite a trans shooter having recently killed six people at a Christian school in Nashville, Bud Light decided to link up with Dylan Mulvaney, one of the most prominent trans activists in the country. Mulvaney's face was instantly slapped on the side of a Bud Light can, and their customer base reacted with disgust. They launched an extended boycott that lost the company more than $27 billion in market value. Celebrities like Kid Rock filmed themselves shooting cases of Bud Light, starting a viral social media trend of angry consumers disposing of the beer in creative ways.

Anheuser-Busch refused to apologize to its customers, instead sheepishly fending off accusations of "transphobia" from progressives who felt they had not done enough to protect Mulvaney. It is hard to understate the level of public relations nightmare Anheuser-Busch brought upon itself. Any man who was caught asking for a Bud Light at the bar was mocked relentlessly by his friends for ordering the "trans beer." The drink of choice for millions of Americans became a punchline with its core demographic overnight. Retailers and bars reduced their inventory or removed the beer entirely.

This series of events makes absolutely no sense when viewed through the simple lens of free-market capitalism. If a cabal of Anheuser-Busch's enemies wanted to take the company down, they could not do better than placing Dylan Mulvaney's face on a Bud Light can. Why did this happen? The answer is that the individual managers inside Anheuser-Busch do not, in fact, act in the interest of the company or its shareholders. Each of these managers knows that they will eventually need to get another job to advance their careers. Some will do so by moving up inside the organization, but most will move to other companies. Skill sets inside the managerial class are largely interchangeable and bureaucrats freely move between employers to climb the ladder. Losing market value is not great, but betraying the managerial class itself is far more deleterious to your employment prospects.

The decision makers inside Bud Light thus care more about their own social status and career opportunities than they do about the goals of the organization they operate. Decoupling the interests of those decision makers from the costs of their decisions inevitably incentivizes behavior in direct opposition to the wellbeing of the institution they were originally designated to oversee.

Bureaucracies, by their very nature, will grow until they create this level of abstraction.

While this phenomenon is easy to observe inside corporations, it arises just as reliably at the level of civilizations. When nations are founded, it is usually by a particular people, an extended tribe or clan seeking to establish ownership over their destiny by taking political organization into their own hands. When a state is young, it does not require much written law or regulation because the expected social behaviors are deeply tied to the religion, traditions, and folkways of the people. The culture is still very closely connected to the animating metaphysical spirit that founded the nation in the first place. Large organizations are nonexistent and extended families tend to handle the bulk of social obligations like education and care for the elderly. Churches and other community organizations may offer assistance to fill the gaps, but everyone is required to have skin in the game.

As nations grow in territory and size, they must also grow in complexity. Territorial acquisition through either conquest or diplomacy means the incorporation of new peoples into the society that do not share the history and traditions of the founding population. These new inhabitants can be incorporated successfully, but they must assimilate to the new culture. That means constitutions and laws that dictate expected behaviors and norms must be created so new arrivals can understand what is required. The new inhabitants often lack extended clans rooted deeply in the folkways of the host culture, which means community organizations and churches need to expand and take up the slack.

As the nation scales in size, the transmission of its culture becomes more abstract and the complexity of its supporting organizations increases dramatically. Ways of being that were once absorbed through generational contact must be condensed into lists of values that are read out to new arrivals during civics classes. Social needs, like education and care for the elderly, become vast projects too complex for individual community organizations, so the state builds large bureaucracies to manage them instead. Every aspect of society gets removed further and further from its founding purpose.

Western liberal democracies have now become little more than a network of impersonal bureaucratic organizations, while their governments now bear all the trademark signs of bureaucratic drift that Conquest warned about in his three laws. Modern states seek to expand their influence and increase their scale by implementing these vast bureaucracies, but in the process they completely separate the incentive structure of the managers from the populations they were originally designed to serve. The lack of skin in the game means the managerial elite are far removed from the consequences of their decisions and can instead focus entirely on their need to acquire power inside their organizations.

The nature of dialectical reconstruction drives those seeking power to focus on progressive social causes to create division and reap the benefits. This means that in a society that is entirely constructed of managerial bureaucracies, every organization is designed to rip itself apart through an endless loop of left-wing ideological purity spirals. The bad news is the total state was an inevitable consequence of adopting the social structures that allowed civilizations to scale well beyond their natural capacity. The good news is they are hardwired to self-destruct.

CHAPTER 10

Why the Total State Is Doomed

The preceding chapters have not painted a rosy picture. The march of the total state has been presented as relentless while the mechanisms championed to restrain power have failed to halt its advance. Managerial bureaucracy has become the default structure for social organization, destroying all competing spheres of influence and homogenizing all cultures in an effort to manufacture a more compliant populace.

But there is good news. The foundation of the total state is fundamentally unstable. The power of the managerial elite is based on a false vision of humanity that will collapse under sufficient strain. The total state is doomed to ruin, though, as we will see, that downfall will come with its own consequences.

Before we look at how the total state will fall, we need to better understand how ruling classes throughout history are either renewed or replaced. As we discussed previously, Italian political theorist and sociologist Vilfredo Pareto observed that all ruling classes contain a balance of what he referred to as residues, and of those residues, two types are most prominent: foxes and lions. Foxes are crafty and clever. They focus on combinations to create new ideas and solutions. Lions are strong and brave. They focus on the preservation of identity and tradition.

A ruling class is always present, but no healthy society has a totally static set of elites. The conditions a nation faces are constantly shifting, and the composition of a ruling elite must also constantly adapt in order to meet new challenges. During a time of war or physical danger, a society needs an elite composed primarily of lions to train and lead an army into battle. At a time of peace, economic and logistical concerns may require solutions that only foxes can provide. The elite class will always have some mixture of both skill sets, but it must be fluid enough to adapt its composition to the needs of the civilization over which it rules.

Aristocracy is an inescapable fact of human organization. Just as there will always be a ruling class, that ruling class will always seek to pass on its power and privilege to its heirs. Whether fox or lion, all members of the ruling elite grant preference to their friends, families, and other members of their class. This means no ruling elite is ever completely open to the elevation of common members of the society into its ranks. This preference serves a practical purpose. Those descended from the ruling class are more likely to have the natural ability and receive the skills and training necessary to lead. A completely open ruling class leads to instability, as those of dubious qualification engage in a never-ending struggle for power and dominance. But even if a totally open elite were desirable, it never exists for long, as the drive to benefit one's lineage is one of the most powerful human instincts.

While aristocracy is unavoidable, an elite must change over time to reflect the needs of the society, so every healthy ruling class allows some method by which new members may be elevated into positions of leadership. There will always be those among the ruled who are capable and ambitious, able to bring new skills and solutions to bear on the problems currently facing their civilization. In some societies, aristocrats adopt exceptional members of the lower class. In others, the church or military sort and elevate those of extraordinary talent. In many Western nations today, educational attainment and financial success are the ladders by which exceptional individuals ascend to the ruling elite. Yet no matter what mechanism it uses, any ruling elite must strike a balance between the persistence of its own dominant minority and the circulation of capable individuals into its ranks.

The temptation to close the ranks of the elite is great, as it allows for a more extreme concentration of power and wealth among those who rule. In the past, such consolidation may have been based on blood or religion; today it is more likely to be ideological. But in either case, an elite that decides to limit access will always set itself on a path to ruin. Over time, a closed elite will degenerate as it limits or completely ceases the flow of new talent into the ruling class.

As Pareto says, "In virtue of class-circulation, the governing elite is always in a state of slow and continuous transformation. It flows on like a river, never being today what it was yesterday. From time to time sudden and violent disturbances occur. There is a flood — the river overflows its banks. Afterward the new governing elite again resumes its slow transformation. The flood has subsided, and the river is again flowing normally in its wonted bed. Revolutions come about through accumulations in the higher strata of society — either because of a slowing down in class-circulation or from other causes — of decadent elements no longer possessing the residues suitable for keeping them in power, and shrinking from the use of force; while meantime in the lower strata of society elements of superior quality are coming to the fore, possessing residues suitable for exercising the functions of government and willing enough to use force."[1]

A closed elite dooms itself in a myriad of ways. It degenerates and becomes decadent as those chosen purely out of nepotism become surer of their right to rule. It loses any connection to the ruled as its interactions become increasingly insular and it grows disdainful of the lower classes. All the while, it denies itself access to those who would naturally rise to leadership and balance that needed mixture. This leads to an extreme imbalance of foxes and lions, as one residue becomes overrepresented in a nepotistic elite that favors only those of the same disposition.

---

1   Pareto, *Compendium of General Sociology*, p. 279.

At the same time, those gifted and ambitious individuals who have been denied entrance into the elite do not just disappear. Some will give up their quest for elevation, but many will become disgruntled and seek alternative avenues of power. A dedicated counter-elite will grow in institutions that become societal pressure points, seeking to leverage the increasingly alienated masses against the sclerotic and indifferent ruling class.

It is a common misconception that regimes fall when they become overbearing and totalitarian. Regimes fall when they have grown weak and decadent, unable to control the population through the manipulation of the fox or the force of the lion. When elites close themselves off to the natural circulation of new talent, they grow soft, and those denied access can suddenly disrupt the status quo.

Pareto uses the Greek civilizations of Athens and Sparta as examples of societies dominated by fox and lion residues respectively. While the openness and cleverness of the Athenian leaders allowed for great flourishing in economics, art, and philosophy, those qualities also resulted in factionalism, scheming, and political plotting that weakened the unity of the people and made it difficult for them to persist through the Peloponnesian Wars. Sparta's legendary military tradition gave it an incredible ability to endure adversity and maintain unity, but the failure of its elite to produce an empire or great cultural advancements meant it could not adapt to rapid change and eventually faded in the shadow of those who could.

According to Pareto, over time, most elite classes tend to see a concentration of fox residues and a waning of lion residues. This leads to a loss of religiosity, identity, and martial prowess among the ruling class, which starts to select primarily for cunning and deception inside its own ranks. A healthy circulation of elites will temper this tendency, replenishing the ruling class with a supply of capable leaders who are still religious, patriotic, and connected to the people. A closed elite filled with foxes will lose connection to both its identity and the people, creating an external surplus of capable lions who have been denied access and ultimately the kind of societal pressure that leads to more sudden and dramatic change.

Pareto writes, "By opening only to those individuals who betray faith and conscience in order to procure the benefits which the plutocracy so lavishly bestows on those who devote themselves to its service, it acquires elements that in no way serve to supply it with the things it most needs. It does, to be sure, deprive the opposition of a few of its leaders, and that is very helpful to it; but it acquires nothing to replenish its own inner strength. So long as cunning and corruption serve, it is likely to keep winning victories, but it falls very readily if violence and force chance to interpose."[2]

A wise ruling class will strike a balance between protecting its own power and allowing for the circulation of new elites. A ruling class that succumbs to the temptation to completely close its ranks does not escape this

---

2   Pareto, *Compendium of General Sociology*, p. 372.

reality, but only delays it and ensures the circulation will be more severe.

Even if the circulation does eventually take place through a more dramatic event like a cultural or violent revolution, Pareto reminds us that it is very rare for an elite to be completely replaced. The ruling class may be heavily disrupted by a sudden surge of foxes or lions, but usually a large element of the previous elite persists in the new arrangement. For Pareto, the story of a civilization is the story of its ruling elites, and while that elite may always be in some degree of flux, the religion, art, and culture that define a society are inextricably linked to the elite class that guides it.

Pareto's model gives us a valuable overview of how and why a ruling class is displaced, but it is only an outline. Each civilizational form has its own specific political structure and character that determines the unique selection pressures that drive its circulation of elites. Late-stage Western liberal democracy is clearly a form that becomes dominated by fox-style elites and chokes on the consequences. Its reliance on managerial power has allowed it to dominate the modern era and assemble the total state through manipulation and soft power, but this also creates critical vulnerabilities that inevitably cause its demise.

In his book *After Virtue*, Alasdair MacIntyre observes that liberal philosophy had mostly given up on determining metaphysical truth through reason due to the general failure of that project. As we observed earlier with the help of Carl Schmitt, liberalism instead swept the metaphysical problems, the larger conflict of moral visions, into the broom closet in the hopes of creating a system of cooperation that ignored those questions. Liberalism promised to replace the existential conflict of the friend/enemy distinction with free markets, democracy, and proceduralism. Once all metaphysical questions had been purged, the only objective good liberalism really had left to pursue was efficiency. This is where the managerial class and their massified institutions became essential to the project.

This is the reason managers became the key building blocks of modern liberal society. Bureaucratic management is supposed to offer a morally neutral increase in efficiency. The telos for the organizations they operate is not the explicit domain of the manager. What is the goal of the organization? Is it a worthy goal, one towards which society should be directing its energies? These are not issues for managers to decide. Managers, at least in theory, exist to make processes within institutions more efficient. But as we have seen, there is no such thing as a morally neutral institution, be it a government or a corporation. Managers have beliefs, goals, and desires, all of which act on the decisions they make.

MacIntyre points out that, just as managers cannot really be objective or neutral, neither can the efficiency they generate. Effectiveness and efficiency cannot be separated from a system that is forever nudging people into predictable patterns of behavior. Since this has become a skill set central to the functioning of the current liberal paradigm, managers have claimed a large amount of authority in our society. Some might hesitate to describe this authority as moral, but it is clear that efficiency has become its own prescriptive argument, and moral decisions are made on that basis. This creates an implicit value judgment that defines the hierarchy inside our civilization.

MacIntyre finds these implicitly moral claims dubious for a number of reasons, not the least of which is that most layers of management do not provide the miracle of efficiency that they promise. The value of expertise does exist in a number of fields. Its power cannot be denied when it comes to a number of critical advancements. But on the back of those advancements, the justification for an almost limitless growth of managerial bureaucracy has been constructed. Both James Burnham and Samuel Francis would recognize that managers are essential for the operation of massified organizations, but MacIntyre asserts that most modern bureaucracy is simply a product of the cancer-like growth of the managerial class and does not actually produce notable increases in efficiency. These layers of bureaucratic management exist only for the purpose of facilitating power.

Writes McIntyre, "It is the gap between the generalized notion of effectiveness and the actual behavior that is open to managers which suggests that the social uses of the notion are other than they purport to be. That the notion is used to sustain and extend the authority and power of managers is not of course in question; but its use in connection with those tasks derives from the belief that managerial authority and power are justified because managers possess an ability to put skills and knowledge to work in the service of achieving certain ends. But what if effectiveness is part of a masquerade of social control rather than a reality? What if effectiveness were a quality widely imputed to managers and bureaucrats both by themselves and others, but in fact a quality which rarely exists apart from this imputation? . . . What would it be like if social control were indeed a masquerade?"

MacIntyre then proposes a possibility: "what we are oppressed by is not power, but impotence; that one key reason why the presidents of large corporations do not, as some radical critics believe, control the United States is that they do not even succeed in controlling their own corporation; that all too often, when imputed organizational skill and power are deployed and the desired effect follows, all that we have witnessed is the same kind of sequence as that to be observed when a clergyman is fortunate enough to pray for rain just before the unpredicted end of a drought; that the levers of power- one of managerial expertise's key metaphors- produce effects unsystematically and too often only coincidentally related to the effect of which their users boast."[3]

Whether real, or merely projected to secure power, as stated before, managers rely on their ability to coerce people into compliant patterns of behavior in order to produce their promised efficiency. Spontaneity and unpredictable responses thus must be suppressed or

---

3	MacIntyre, *After Virtue*, p.75.

eliminated. However, MacIntyre goes on to note that increasing predictability past a certain point dooms an organization, eliminating its ability to seek novel solutions outside its well-defined and optimized system.

MacIntyre again: "Since organizational success and organizational predictability exclude one another, the project of creating a wholly or largely predictable organization committed to creating a wholly or largely predictable society is doomed and doomed by the facts about social life. Totalitarianism of a certain kind, as imagined by Aldous Huxley or George Orwell, is therefore impossible. What the totalitarian project will always produce will be a kind of rigidity and inefficiency which may contribute in the long run to its defeat. We need to remember, however, the voices from Auschwitz and Gulag Archipelago which tell us just how long that long run is."[4]

The indispensable utility of the managerial class is, to MacIntyre, an illusion projected to justify power. This may be an overstatement, as managers are at some level an essential part of the massified way of being that has come to dominate the modern world, but his point about the diminishing returns of compounding bureaucratic layers is well taken. It is clear that much of the managerial apparatus creates no material benefit, and that the totalitarian system it births is ultimately doomed to fail. The extreme flattening of culture and tradition required to generate such a level of control contains the seeds of

---

4   MacIntyre, *After Virtue*, p.106.

the regime's destruction. Centralization is always power's natural goal, but the vast bureaucracy that is required demands ever-increasing levels of predictability, and therefore, as power gets nearer and nearer to its goal, it necessarily renders the system sterile, unable to produce new ideas and solutions. In the end, the regime will only be able to more efficiently manage its own decline.

Western civilization is already encountering the limits of modern total state. Both Joseph de Maistre and Carl Schmitt believed that political theology was inescapable and that governments will always be patterned after a relationship with the divine. Liberal democracy made several key promises, but the most important was the miracle of progress. Material abundance, a longer lifespan, and technological innovation were, in theory, the products of a society that had abandoned the backward and superstitious world of enchantment and tradition for the scientifically managed utopia of modernity.

As the world went from the horse to the train to the car to the airplane, and as lifespans extended into the seventies, it seemed, for a brief time at least, like the miracle really could go on forever. This progress, however, was not without cost. As we have seen, a fundamental transformation of society was required to create the structure that undergirds the modern world, and while the managerial system is attempting to globalize in an effort to outrun its own limitations, this strategy is already slowing down.

Globalization brought new markets and a vast network of massified production, raw materials, and cheap labor, enabling a just-in-time delivery system that maximized efficiency. In theory, everything can be manufactured at its cheapest price because materials are delivered to their point of production and end products are delivered to their consumers without the cost of storage. The site of production is no longer restricted to a specific geographic location in relation to either raw materials or the end user, so the cheapest labor and materials can always be selected regardless of the location of the consumer. Loss of efficiency due to the storage of either raw materials or finished inventory is reduced because materials arrive just in time for production and finished products are shipped out just in time to meet consumer demand. This system works beautifully so long as goods and labor are allowed to flow without restriction or interruption. But this requires a high degree of competence and coordination, which is increasingly difficult for the managerial class to produce.

Once again, the COVID pandemic provides an excellent example of the system under stress. Labor was massively disrupted as many fell sick and the rest were locked down. International shipping became a logistical nightmare as fear of spreading the pandemic made routine transportation a health hazard. Americans discovered that, due to an overriding drive to increase efficiency and profit margins, production of key medical machinery like respirators and prescription drugs like antibiotics had been outsourced to China, the country that had served as the origin of the virus. In the name of managerial efficiency, the United States had not only made itself vulnerable to the spread of a pandemic from China, but had made itself reliant on that same nation for the treatment of that same pandemic. That nation also happens to be the United States' primary global competitor. Most concerningly, no lesson has been learned. No serious effort has been made to transfer production to more local and secure facilities. America remains just as reliant on its most serious geopolitical foe as ever.

A similar disruption in the global supply chain can be seen in response to the recent war between Russia and Ukraine. NATO nations, led by the United States, assumed they would be able to use economic pressure to bring a swift end to Vladimir Putin's invasion. Instead, it was only underscored how dependent the West had made itself on Russia for energy, fertilizer, and other essential resources. Instead of global financial markets bringing Russia to its knees, Western nations were rocked by skyrocketing food and energy prices. As a result, many have now agreed to shift their currencies in order to buy oil from Russia, while the famous petrodollar, the reserve currency of the world that has kept the American economy on top for decades, is in danger of losing its status. An international logistics system that seemed destined to spread its hegemonic influence across the globe is now showing how easily it can be disrupted by incompetence, hubris, and the brute facts of human nature.

Ultimately, the total state will fail because widely different peoples spread across vast distances cannot, and will not, be governed as one unified whole. The total state may have dissolved the social fabric, destroyed meaningful spiritual connection, and eliminated hard property in order to make its subjects easier to rule, but it has also made the nation's human capital sadder, less healthy, and less competent in the process.

Americans are watching their lifespans shorten, mental illness surge, and family formation dive off a cliff. In the effort to engineer more compliant subjects, the total state has created a populace incapable of doing the one thing humans are supposed to strive for: living a life full of meaningful accomplishments and connections. Middle America has been hollowed out in order to access wider consumer markets and cheaper labor in nations like India and China, but those countries are not infinitely malleable either and attempts to base the global network on their continued social engineering will inevitably fail. As Samuel Francis pointed out, humans are not interchangeable and programmable widgets, and the assumption that they can be engineered into a universal, easily managed mass is a fatal error.

Writes Francis, "The 'open society' ideal of the soft elite, allowing it to sanction and subvert non- and anti-managerial authorities and values and to manipulate and accelerate ideas and values that enhance its own dominance, prevents the formulation or enforcement of an ascetic and solidarist orthodoxy that could satisfy psychic and social needs in ways that technocratic, hedonistic, and cosmopolitan ideologies cannot. The soft managerial regime, in its ideological illusion that human beings are creatures of their social and historical environment and can be ameliorated through the managed manipulation of the environment, has only dispersed authority and values and sought to manipulate their fragments. The soft elite does not recognize–and cannot recognize, given its worldview and the material and political interests on which its worldview is based– that immutable elements of human nature constrain the possibilities of amelioration and necessitate attachment to the concrete social and historical roots of moral values and meaning, at the expense of the mythologies of cosmopolitan dispersion and hedonistic indulgence."[5]

The materialistic and hedonistic pseudo-religion used by the total state to liquify cultures and produce more efficiently managed bureaucracies has no staying power. The ideological need to sever man from the transcendent abolishes that which truly makes him human. The posthuman future is not one of wondrous space travel but the slow decline of a society no longer capable of innovation, creativity, or even general maintenance. Each generation of managerial elites becomes more powerful by creating more uniformity, limiting options, and standardizing thought. The ability to maintain systems fades, while individuals become too atomized and hedonistic to sacrifice on behalf of the future. The attempt to construct the perfect posthuman managerial subject capable of integrating into a global society dooms itself by ignoring essential truths that are both material and spiritual in nature. As G. K. Chesterton rightly observed,

5   Francis, *Leviathan and Its Enemies*, p.682.

"Every high civilization decays by forgetting obvious things."

The Tower of Babel is not an engineering problem. It is a pattern repeating itself across human history: the hubris of a power centralizing in the hopes of reaching heaven only to collapse under its own weight and, perhaps, a nudge from the divine. While there is hope in knowing this corrupt system will not last forever, Alasdair MacIntyre was wise to warn us against forgetting the terrible costs it can inflict in the meantime.

CHAPTER 11

The Only Way Out Is Through

While it is comforting to know the total state will fail, we still have to live in a world where they continue to hold power. The question becomes: How do we weather this storm and emerge on the other side?

Two strategies are currently popular among those who oppose the total state, but both suffer from the same flaw.

Conservatives would like to return to the 1950s, the decade in which America became remarkably affluent and emerged as the premier world power. They acknowledge a lack of religiosity as the key factor in America's moral degradation, but tend to become uncomfortable when anyone questions how massified social structures like corporations may have contributed to that fact. Conservatives understand the collapse of family and church as a central problem but rarely look at structural factors, preferring to lay blame solely at the feet of those who failed to embrace those institutions. Conservatives treat the Constitution as infallible even though the total state managed to assemble itself despite the document's famous protections against tyranny. The Constitution is seen not as a document formalizing the folkways and traditions of a nation, but as a universal system of government whose proper application will bring freedom and prosperity to whatever people it governs.

Conservatives believe that liberal democracy, as it is set out in the Constitution, works perfectly, and if something has gone wrong, it can only be because the document has been subverted or improperly applied. They are quick to remind us that the United States is a republic and not a democracy. That was true once, of course, but if you ask a conservative which group should lose the franchise or when we should repeal the direct election of senators, they will look at you like you have grown a second and third head.

The conservative solution to the total state is best personified in the attempt to call a convention of the states. Article V of the Constitution allows for thirty-four states to call for a convention, which can then draft constitutional amendments for ratification. Because the convention of states would take place outside the corrupted bureaucracy of Washington, D.C., it could entertain ideas no established politician would, or so the theory goes. This process could be used to patch up critical ambiguities that have been exploited by courts, legislators, and federal bureaucrats. The Constitution would thus be restored to its position of primacy and the American government would again be constrained by masterful checks and balances.

The issues with this strategy are legion. It does not address any of the problems laid out by de Maistre, Yarvin, or Mosca. It ignores Schmitt's explanation of why democratic politics will inevitably progress towards a total state. It is not simply technical flaws in the Constitution that have left constitutional rule in shambles, and the patching of a few leaks will not right the ship. The conservative approach is not one that seeks a new path through a difficult present, but instead hopes to escape difficult truths by reenacting past glories.

Video blogger David Greene has compared the attempt to resurrect the Constitution to the phenomenon of the Ghost Dance in the late nineteenth century.[1] American Indians at that time were watching their way of life disappear as a foreign culture forced them into ever-smaller reservations and made their traditions increasingly difficult to practice. Some of these tribes came to believe that by participating in certain rituals, they could reconnect with the spirits of their ancestors and bring about the restoration of their once great nations. In many ways, the Ghost Dance did embody what had once made these tribes both vital and powerful. The dance gathered so many warriors that the United States sent a large force to investigate the Lakota, who were performing it. Some of the Lakota performed the Ghost Dance, believing it would shield them from the bullets of the American

---

1   https://www.youtube.com/watch?v=1jDOMmk3N_A&t=1s &ab_channel=TheDistributist.

soldiers. The ensuing clash resulted in the famous massacre at Wounded Knee.

The Ghost Dance might have had a connection to the past, but it never had any hope of defeating the US military or restoring the Lakota to greatness. Those who performed it ignored reality and made themselves easy targets in the process. Likewise, despite its impressive legacy, the US Constitution does not, and cannot, restrain the total state. The founding fathers were deeply inspiring, but the problem of tyranny has spread far beyond anything they ever envisioned. Conservatives cannot continue to Ghost Dance, or they will meet a similar fate.

There is an additional question of character that must be acknowledged. American conservatives love to quote John Adams, who said, "Our constitution was made only for a moral and religious people. It is wholly inadequate to the government of any other." But they rarely consider the deeper implications of what Adams was saying. If the Constitution is only meant for a moral and religious people, and Americans are no longer moral or religious, then the Constitution is no longer adequate to govern them. Whether you believe the citizens of the West were already degenerating, or whether you believe the total state used social engineering to strip away their virtue, the uncomfortable truth remains.

Conservatives often respond that a return to real self-government through constitutional restoration will revive the American character and allow the populace to once again embrace virtue, but this inverts causality.

Liberty is the fruit of virtue; virtue is not the fruit of liberty. Even if conservatives could restore proper constitutional government and patch the holes that caused the ship to sink in the first place, they would still be using it to govern a people for which John Adams himself declared it inadequate.

The second popular strategy for opposing the total state comes from those who label themselves classical or "non-woke" liberals. These are liberals who previously might have identified themselves as moderate progressives, but for one reason or another have found themselves forced out of the ruling coalition. One can usually hear them parroting the familiar refrain, "I didn't leave the left, the left left me," while explaining how radical the movement they once championed has become.

The total state has accelerated its advance by demolishing both civil liberties and social norms, and the speed at which those barriers have been breached has left many who once sat comfortably inside the friend/enemy distinction shocked at the hostility they now face for holding what were previously acceptable opinions. Anti-war leftists, free speech advocates, and gay marriage proponents now find themselves ejected from the Left if they are not supportive of new agendas like critical race theory, the mutilation of children under trans ideology, and the state persecution of dissidents.

These liberal castoffs find themselves with no allies to their left, so they are forced to make common cause with conservatives. This coalition is one of convenience—the liberal castoffs are not fans of their new allies, and have an even more disastrous approach to opposing the total state. These progressive refugees see nothing wrong with their prior positions, blaming instead the radical advance of the revolution that left them behind. Restrictive moral particulars, traditional social institutions, and natural hierarchies are still treated as outdated.

Liberals who find themselves in this position wish to return to the 1990s instead of the 1950s. They would like to maintain all of the cultural developments they see as social progress. They wish simply to roll back liberalism to a past patch, the one where the illusion of neutral institutions and free speech was maintained. The subversion of the progressive movement by Marxism is usually blamed for the sudden woke radicalization of the ideology they once supported.

Alienated leftists hope that once this subversion is purged, everyone can return to the previously ideal liberal consensus. This approach assumes the presidency of Barack Obama was the end of history, the final answer to all questions of moral progress and political organization. These liberal refugees can never acknowledge that much of the framework they championed led to their current situation. Their disagreements with the ideology of the total state are of degree and not kind, and this dooms any attempt at opposition.

The truth is, and this is a very difficult truth for even me to admit, that there is no going back. No regime is eternal, history is not over, and every epoch eventually gives way to the next. Constitutional liberal democracy had a relatively short but admittedly impressive run, conquering the globe and overseeing some of the most radical changes in human history. But its time has drawn to an end. The managerial elite have woven the institutions of liberal democracy into the total state and now operate their bureaucratic theocracy while wearing the old regime like a skinsuit.

The preceding chapters have outlined how that process took place and why constitutional liberal states were unable to recognize, much less arrest, the transformation that was occurring inside their civilizations. What we are experiencing is not simply the failure of one or two aspects of the existing system that can be easily reformed. Likewise, the rise of the total state was not just a cunning subversion that can be accounted for and protected against going forward. Progressivism did in many ways subvert our existing system, but only because it was already ripe for such a takeover.

Liberal democracy made assumptions about human nature that were false. It outran the consequences for a long time because it was able to amass an unprecedented amount of wealth and power, but eventually the bill always comes due. Constitutions are not eternal guardians of the political will and states do not become objective and self-governing machines simply because rules get written down on a piece of paper. Man has not moved beyond either religion or politics. Questions of faith and sovereignty will continue to sit at the core of the human experience, just as they always have. Matters of meaning, identity, and existential conflict cannot be

removed by the promise of cold objective reason and credentialed experts.

All of these assumptions are dangerously false, but
they are also core to modern liberal democracy as we
understand it. Our entire political and economic system
is tied directly to beliefs that can no longer sustain the
weight of that system. The managers of the total state
have warped and conditioned human nature, pushing
rootless and atomized individuals to their limits, but the
structures that were designed to squeeze every last drop
of efficiency from the homogenized masses are already
showing signs of failure.

The problem we face is regime complete: There is no
simple trick that can return us to a neutral and objective
liberal consensus that never existed. We sit at the edge
of a transition amid a historical cycle that repeats itself
over and over again. Empires rise, power centralizes,
and civilization is pushed to its limits, before the entire
structure collapses under its own weight. Managerialism
is a relatively new social order that has taken the process further than it has ever traveled before, but it's
still doomed by the truths of human nature it seeks to
destroy. We cannot reassert the liberalism of the 1990s,
or the 1950s, or even the 1790s. The only way out is
through.

The question is not how to avoid the failures of
our liberal democracy but how best to navigate what
has become inevitable. Predicting the future is a dangerous thing for any author, and almost always leaves
him looking foolish. But given the importance of what's

happening, I'd like to consider three possibilities for the future of the total state. We will look at each in turn.

The first possibility is that the unprecedented wealth and power that the total state has accumulated allows it to hobble along, while the quality of life of its citizens declines more or less in perpetuity. This is the least likely of all outcomes for the reasons explained in the previous chapter. The total state's flawed assumptions about human nature are disastrous and the critical points of failure in the globalist project are already starting to show. It is difficult to imagine the current decentralized regime lasting thirty years, much less three hundred.

There are regimes that fall from first-world to third-world status while the current management stays in power, but they also can't be the world hegemon. The might of the US military has created a Pax Americana that is essential to the global expansion of the total state's managerial apparatus. Even if those who live under the total state were to sit quietly by amid slow-motion collapse, the incredibly expensive and complicated endeavor of maintaining a global military empire cannot gradually degrade without serious consequences.

Nations like China and Russia, which do not wish to play a subservient role to Western liberal democracies, are already testing the system and discovering weaknesses. If the United States and its satellite nations continue to demonstrate an inability to maintain their hegemony, then more countries are likely to flee a sinking ship and seek viable alternatives. In this scenario, it seems incredibly unlikely that the West would be able to continue its globalist expansion unopposed. Anything is possible, but I do not think this is the future those who are seeking to come out on the other side need to prepare for.

The second possibility is the entrance of a strongman who can reassert order and return competency to the degenerating managerial elite. As we discussed in the previous chapter, Pareto explains the instability that can arise when a government is dominated entirely by fox-style elites who suppress lion-style elites. While the might of the US military is deployed abroad to ensure the stability of global trade and communications, at home, liberal democracies are very hesitant to deploy violence. Make no mistake: Western governments can and do turn their own security apparatuses against their citizens when necessary, but they do so uncomfortably and incompetently, and it shows.

Historically, when governments prove incapable of providing safety, security, and economic stability, while also being unable to manage the populace, citizens look for competent and decisive leadership to cut through the decrepit bureaucracy and return order. Caesarism, as it is often called, is a recurring pattern across civilizations and there is no reason to think Western democracies are immune. The Caesar figure usually emerges from, or has direct support from, the military, as this is the only way for suppressed lion elites to take back control from the bureaucratic stranglehold of the foxes. While this may seem far-fetched to some, it is always dangerous to pretend modernity makes one immune to the forces of history. When jobs are scarce, the streets are unsafe, and people find themselves without hope for a brighter future, most will be happy to find someone who can make the trains run on time.

While Caesar figures traditionally conjure up the image of a military dictator, that is not the only way the pattern manifests itself. The United States has its own tradition of imperial presidencies, including those of Andrew Jackson, Abraham Lincoln, and Franklin Delano Roosevelt. While neither Lincoln nor Roosevelt was a military man, both managed to use emergency powers to suspend large swaths of the Constitution and bend the government to their will. Both transformed the United States while ignoring almost all constitutional restrictions, and there is no reason to believe this couldn't happen again.

The United States has an almost sacrosanct tradition of civilian leadership over its armed forces, which should make it difficult for a military strongman to secure power. Yet the fact that generalship, something that once stood as an eminent qualification for executive office, seems to bear little to no weight at all among today's voters speaks volumes. The truth is that most generals today are more fox than lion, chosen for their ability to efficiently operate the large bureaucratic organizations of the Pentagon rather than lead men into battle. Modern Western generals are not opponents of the managerial class, but members of that class who work towards the goals of the total state. In truth, the United States seems far more likely to see another Lincoln or FDR before it gets a Francisco Franco.

The modern age is one of money power, and Caesar is just as likely to be a billionaire CEO as a military dictator. This is the solution political theorist Curtis Yarvin advocates: the election of a visionary CEO granted the powers of a monarch to return competence and stability. In Yarvin's future, the CEO king would restore sanity by eliminating the democratic element from the managerial regime, removing the need for mass propaganda and obsessive enforcement of the progressive theocracy. This would also eliminate the necessity for the obsessive denial of reality that currently plagues the total state and would allow mass institutions to return to efficient operation once they have been purged of ideology. The masses would no longer need to be hyperfixated on every facet of politics because, with their access to the franchise removed, they would no longer be relentlessly propagandized by elites who wished to maintain their control. Schmitt identified the democratic element as the main driver of the total state, so Yarvin is definitely onto something. But his CEO king still fails to address a major problem: the leviathan managerial apparatus itself.

It is true that the liberal denial of human nature caused it to obscure the friend/enemy distinction in favor of a kind of cold civil war whose rules were already rigged. Democracy required propaganda to be spread across every realm of society if the ruling class was to maintain power, and removing this incentive for quasi-religious mind control would doubtless be a positive step. But the problem is not simply one of ideological zealotry driven by the mechanism of popular sovereignty. Power, as we learned from Bertrand de Jouvenel, is an arms race towards centralization. The state must collapse competing social spheres in order to expand and consolidate its reach. The total state has already decimated the independent structures of family, religion, and community, and other nations must keep pace with this centralization or risk becoming vassals of a superpower with which they cannot compete.

In addition, while the progressive "secular" faith may have begun as a way to circumvent constitutional restrictions and control the democratic process, it has now become instrumental to the larger project of managerial domination. Managers need a homogenous, predictable, and compliant populace in order to efficiently operate the large bureaucracies that allow for the massification of society. The removal of progressive orthodoxy will reduce the number of absurd fictions these organizations must entertain, which will undoubtedly increase their efficiency and longevity. But they will still run into the same root problem: society is not meant to scale infinitely. Humans were not designed to exist in or be governed by a global community. In order to continue to operate, massified bureaucracies will need to continue liquidating cultural differences, destroying moral particularities, and making subjects entirely dependent on their system. Even if stripped of its progressive theocratic elements, the total state would still be fighting against core truths about human identity and wellbeing. The Tower of Babel will eventually collapse under its own weight.

The final scenario I will address is the one I think is most likely, and that gives us the best look at a way forward: The total state is doomed and its collapse will likely be gradual. As different systems are pushed to their limits and begin to falter, the total state's control will become more tenuous.

When the government is strong and capable, improving material conditions and delivering prosperity, most are happy to go along, even if their senses of community and spiritual well-being are harmed in the process. But the total state is failing to deliver the miracle of progress while liberal democracies are collapsing before our very eyes. Western nations are losing their capacity to produce and maintain reliable electrical grids. Supply chains that deliver essential goods like fuel, medicine, and food are proving less reliable, and economies have been deeply impacted by expected shortages. Nations that are not sold on the global democratic project have begun testing the West's military hegemony. Eventually, maintaining the core functions of the total state will require more capacity than the managerial bureaucracy is able to deliver.

During the pandemic, many regimes suffered from hubris and faced serious backlash after testing their capacity for both hard and soft power. The fact that the West decided to immediately test that capacity again with a proxy war against Russia demonstrates that its leadership has become completely disconnected from reality. The total state will continue to govern as if it has the ability to compel any behavior, despite the fact that it is doing permanent damage to itself in the process. Our elites see themselves as invincible and cannot imagine a reality that does not bend to their will. This means the regime will continue to pursue its ideological ends without restraint, even as it strains its ability to maintain order to the breaking point.

As the total state becomes more overtly authoritarian and less competent, individuals will flee to regions that are attempting to protect themselves from the fallout. In America, Florida has already seen a massive influx of new residents attempting to escape the insane pandemic regulations of their previous home states. Florida has developed a reputation for standing not just against the biomedical security apparatus but the ideological agenda of the regime. In addition, Florida has maintained a flourishing economy and relatively low crime rate by rejecting progressive dogma around policing and ousting the hostile district attorneys famously elevated by the likes of George Soros to devastate law and order across the country.

So far, the federal government has been unable to punish Florida and its governor, Ron DeSantis, for these transgressions, but his resistance to the total state has also been relatively minor. If a state were to trigger any real crisis of sovereignty by policing its own border or challenging federal law enforcement, a true clash of authority would ensue. So far, governors haven't been bold enough to push past these bright red lines, and even if they were, the central government would likely be competent enough to respond. But this will not be the case forever.

Eventually the total state will become so corrupt that submission to its authority will guarantee noticeable social degradation. It will become so inept that regions will find it easier to ignore its dictates than to follow them. This is not some fantastical vision of the future; it is simply the way most dying empires have gone. The imperial core becomes decadent and incompetent, unable to manage itself much less the outlying provinces, while capable regional leaders push for autonomy. The successful provinces are the ones that take on essential functions that the central authority can no longer reliably provide. The central authority may grumble, but if regional leadership is competently providing services, then it has very little leverage against the governors of these provinces.

The central government would need to send a military force to bring its rogue provinces back into line. Otherwise, if the leadership is incapable of using overwhelming military force or unwilling to endure the horrific backlash that would accompany turning its armed forces on its own people, it will have lost all claim to sovereignty, and other regions will take notice. This is an incredibly high-risk proposition, which is why most decaying central authorities have allowed regional autonomy while maintaining the illusion of sovereignty. No government official ever comes out and announces the empire is over; it just slowly decays as, one by one, regions find it easier to govern themselves than to submit to a central state.

This slow decay has serious geopolitical implications, but they are too vast to examine here and I would be well out of my depth. Historically, the provinces of decaying empires can flourish in their independence; they can also prove incapable of providing the basic functions of a state, or fall under the sway of other powerful political actors. The decay of the total state does not create some utopian world in which each region becomes free and prosperous. For many, it will mean political instability and a reduced standard of living. Things may have been getting progressively worse under the total state, but like an institutionalized prisoner who can no longer survive in the real world, the regions have lost the ability to function without an ever-present master. The United States and the liberal democracies that orbit it serve as the global hegemon, dictating the military and economic terms to every other nation on the planet. With that overbearing structure removed, an endless number of possibilities, both thrilling and horrific, emerge.

These issues will be well beyond the scope of the individual to address, but for those seeking the best way through the collapse of the total state, this regional independence does offer new opportunities. The total state relied on the destruction of competing social spheres and the liquidation of cultural particulars to consolidate power. Lip service was given to a fake and plastic version of diversity, but true cultural and moral differentiation was crushed. Families, communities, churches, and other competing power centers were destroyed or made intentionally weak. As centralized power degrades, these more local and organic forms of social organization will once again have the opportunity to flourish.

Without omnipresent massified bureaucracy, people will be forced to devolve their dependence down to traditional social spheres.

While this relocalization is a positive step towards escaping the total state, many will reject it. Modern man was sold a fictional narrative about liberation and will have a difficult time adjusting to the reassertion of reality. Humans are socially dependent beings. We can be bound to our families, churches, and communities, or we can be bound to the state, but there is no escaping the truth of human dependence. The citizens of liberal democracies went along with the centralization of state power for a reason: it removed the many personal duties and responsibilities that had been placed on them. If the total state is to atrophy and fall away, individuals will once again be required to commit large amounts of time and personal finances to the task of maintaining civilization. Without the total state, communities will have to accept agency over the social necessities once managed by the regime, or slowly die out as they cling to the atomizing and hedonistic lifestyles to which they had become accustomed.

This means that the way through is not some glorious and sudden act of revolution, but the acceptance of responsibility and implementation of careful discipline. This is its own test. As Julius Caesar said, "It is easier to find men who will volunteer to die, than to find those who are willing to endure pain with patience." Our next phase of civilization will select for a very different set of traits, and those who make it through will be those who deny themselves ease and luxury while actively choosing duty and responsibility.

No one chooses to live at the end of an empire, but this is where we find ourselves. We must be the generation that plants trees we will not sit under, the generation willing to sacrifice for a better tomorrow. We must forge a future where true community thrives, where moral and cultural particularity flourish, where people are organic members of a society not mass-produced, where citizens are not socially engineered gears in a bureaucratic machine.

At the individual level, this means forming strong families, taking on the responsibility of caring for our loved ones, and sacrificing some degree of leisure for the duties that come with dependence. Churches will need to return to their status as central community institutions responsible for the charitable functions that have been assumed by the state. Communities will need to take on responsibilities that their regional governments may not have the resources to tackle. Cities and towns will need to take on the character of the America Alexis de Tocqueville admired in the early 1800s: a network of community associations created and maintained by hard-working and dedicated citizens willing to bind themselves together and better the lives of their neighbors.

G. K. Chesterton said, "Men did not love Rome because she was great. She was great because they had loved her." The same will be true after the fall of the total state. The communities that thrive will be those where citizens were willing to once again shoulder the burdens that maintaining civilization demands.

The actions that will matter most in the coming days are local and regional. The election of school board members, sheriffs, and county commissioners who understand what time it is and share the right values is far more important than the machinations of national political parties. Consolidating local power that is capable of resisting the authority of the total state is essential. At first, regional governments will not be able to reject all aspects of centralized power, but they will gradually assume more and more autonomy as the total state decays. As we saw during the pandemic lockdowns, the disposition and competence of a regional government can have a massive impact.

The consolidation of local political power is also likely to cause communities to self-sort. As regional legislatures pass more intensely partisan laws, those who refuse to live under them will vote with their feet. Those who favor mandatory COVID vaccines, abortion, and gender transition surgery for minors will move out of one state and into another, while values become more locally unified and regionally distinct. This consolidation of identity and values will create a more robust sense of community that can stand against a decaying total state. Individuals are more likely to make sacrifices on behalf of a community that is culturally and morally theirs, and protects them from a centralized power that does not share their values or have their wellbeing at heart.

The task ahead is difficult. Transitions from one epoch to another are always fraught with hardship and danger, but they also offer great opportunity. This will be an age that demands great leadership, dedication, and faith. A million small acts of courage and heroism will go unnoticed as people once again form into communities that can survive without the bureaucratic leviathan of massified social organization. The total state will fail in its quest to transform humanity, but that failure will require the return of real existential consequences. The only way out is through.

Bibliography

De Jouvenel, Bertrand. *On Power: The Natural History of Its Growth*. Liberty Fund, 1993.

De Maistre, Joseph. *Major Works*, Vol. 1. Imperium Press, 2021.

Francis, Samuel T. *Leviathan and Its Enemies*. Washington Summit Publishers, 2016.

Land, Nick. *The Dark Enlightenment*. Imperium Press, 2023.

Lewis, C. S. *The Abolition of Man*. MacMillan Publishing Company, 1955.

Madison, James. *The Federalist Papers*. Liberty Fund, 2001.

Mosca, Gaetano. *The Ruling Class*. 3rd ed. McGraw-Hill, 1965.

MacIntyre, Alasdair. *After Virtue*. 2nd ed. University of Notre Dame Press, 1984.

Pareto, Vilfredo. *Compendium of General Sociology*. University of Minnesota Press, 1980.

"Propertarianism, Conservatism, and the 'White Man's Ghost Dance'." YouTube, uploaded by The Distributist, 14 Feb. 2019, www.youtube.com/watch?v=1jDOMmk3N_A&t=1s&ab_channel=TheDistributist.

Schmitt, Carl. *The Concept of the Political*. The University of Chicago Press, 2007.

———. *Political Theology*. The University of Chicago Press, 2005.

Yarvin, Curtis. "A general theory of collaboration." *Gray Mirror*, Substack, 6/11/2020, https://graymirror.substack.com/p/1-a-general-theory-of-collaboration.

INDEX